THE ESSAYS OF
ALICE MEYNELL

ESSAYS

By

ALICE MEYNELL

With an Introduction by
SIR FRANCIS MEYNELL

———

CENTENARY EDITON

———

GREENWOOD PRESS, PUBLISHERS
WESTPORT. CONNECTICUT

CONTENTS

WOMEN AND BOOKS

THE DARLING YOUNG

Most of these Essays are collected and selected from the volumes entitled THE RHYTHM OF LIFE, THE COLOUR OF LIFE, THE SPIRIT OF PLACE, THE CHILDREN, and CERES' RUNAWAY. In addition are "The Seventeenth Century," "Prue," "Mrs. Johnson," and "Madame Roland," here for the first time put into a book.

INTRODUCTION

Alice Meynell, my mother, is my text. What was her context? Of her father, who loved both scholarship and the arts, but, being without ambition, was also without achievement—of her father she wrote after his death:

> "He was not inarticulate, he was only silent. He had an exquisite style from which to refrain. His personality made laws for me; it was a subtle education."

And now as to her mother: Christiana Weller was her mother's name, and she had beauty and talent, and when, in 1844, Dickens heard her play the piano at one of his readings he wrote:

> "I cannot joke about Miss Weller, 'for she is too good; and interest in her (spiritual young creature that she is) has become a sentiment with me. Good God, what a madman I should seem if the incredible feeling I have conceived for that girl could be made plain to anyone."

He said he couldn't joke about Miss Weller. But he could. For he visited her and wrote this jingle in her album:

> I put in a book once by hook and by crook
> The whole race (as I thought) of a feller
> Who happily pleased the town's taste much
>   diseas'd
> And the name of this person was Weller.

I find to my cost that one Weller I lost,
  Cruel destiny so to arrange it!
I love her dear name which has won me some
  fame
    But, Great Heaven, how gladly I'd change
    it!

And it was Dickens who introduced her to his great
friend T. J. Thompson. They fell in love, and married, and had two children—Alice, my mother, and
Elizabeth who won fame as a painter.

My grandparents took their children to Italy,
and brought them up there: and through all my
mother's life it was from Italy—its peasants, its
skies and trees and architecture—that she renewed
and refreshed herself. Italy was her second, her
almost native, land; but for Italian, her second and
almost native tongue, she had no more than an easy
liking, holding it to be too obviously musical in
comparison with what she regarded as the incomparable language for poetry—the English language. My mother disliked intensely being classified
as one of the two, or three, or four (according to
the views of the writer) finest English poetesses.
She offered herself to be criticised, not as a woman
—all-woman as she was—but as a writer. And how
real was the double claim, to be a woman in her
life and a poet and creative writer in her work,
you must judge by two things: first, by the fact
that she enjoyed a most happy married life through
forty-five years and bore eight children; and second, by the essays which are in this volume and
the poetry which I shall discuss in this preface. Of
the essays I will say this—that the writers of her
day (such as Coventry Patmore, George Meredith,
Walter de la Mare, Henry Newboult, Walkley of
The Times, W. E. Henley, William Sharp, Lionel

Johnson) knew her and admired her for her prose much more than for her poems. This was not a choice for them between one form of her expression and the other, but was due to the simple fact that in the middle and greatly fruitful period of her life she wrote few poems and a great deal of what Meredith called her "princely journalism." First in Henley's *Scots Observer* and then anonymously in a weekly article in the *Pall Mall Gazette* she had all reading England as her eager and greatly inquisitive readers. So that when I say "know her for her prose" I speak literal truth, since it was in nearly every case an admiration first for the unknown and unnamed, then for the named but still unknown which caused Meredith and his compeers to seek out her acquaintance and to find and found their love and admiration for her as a woman.

In the 'nineties her girlhood's poems were almost forgotten, her magnificent later poems, written in the last decade of her life, were yet to come. Her contemporaries who first made her fame, it is sad to realise, never knew the full and finest flowering of her mind in those last poems. What they did know was a critic of rare firmness and power of analysis; a writer who could deal with Ruskin's economics or architecture or the women of the 17th century or Gibbon's style in prose, and many another recondite subject with authority, with rich beauty and with a lean wit: and always with an integrity which honoured its subject and honoured also the weight and movement of the English language which she held so dear. This collection of her essays shows her consistency, born not of habit but of just and sensitive free will. Max Beerbohm chided her for the "prunes and prisms" of her style—"ripe prunes and flawless prisms." (Even more he chided those who so admired her that they made her a fashion; these critics condemning her to be, he said, "a substitute for the English sabbath." Style, a conscious style, a proud style, she has indeed; and when one doesn't like style one calls it precious or a mannerism. But, oddly enough, this style is, I think, less marked today than it would have seemed in her day. We expect a difference of idiom in writing of fifty years ago, and any personal idiosyncrasy of hers (I can in fact think only of one her liking for "whereof," "wherefrom" and other such word-saving forms) is merged in the idiosyncrasy of her period. But read her aloud after you have read her to yourself for sense. Read her aloud for the extra meaning, for the over-tone; and I think you will find a new stimulus in her compressions, a new vitality in her quietness, a new pressure in her carefully modulated oratory; and thereafter a new precision in your own use of words.

But here are her essays, speaking for themselves to a generation which happily would rather make its own judgments than take them even from the great writers of the past—which will most certainly not take them from a personally prejudiced middle-distance non-writer like me. For me it is more useful to try to illustrate here not from her present essays but from her absent poetry something of her life and personality.

Alice Meynell was one of the most loved and revered women of her day—a longish day, beginning in 1847 and ending in 1923, when she was seventy-six years old.

Her young poetry was of course musical and sentimental; but her later poetry was packed tight with thought and suggestion. Here is an example of the first—the sonnet which Ruskin said was the most beautiful ever written by a woman. She told me thirty years later: "How much more pleased I should have been if he had said merely 'a good sonnet' ''!

> I must not think of thee; and, tired yet strong,
>> I shun the thought that lurks in all delight—
>> The thought of thee—and in the blue
>>> Heaven's height,
> And in the sweetest passage of a song,
> O just beyond the fairest thoughts that throng
>> This breast, the thought of thee waits hid-
>>> den yet bright;
>> But it must never, never come in sight;
> I must stop short of thee the whole day long.
>
> But when sleep comes to close each difficult
>> day,
>> When night gives pause to the long watch
>>> I keep,
>> And all my bonds I needs must loose
>>> apart,
> Must doff my will as raiment laid away,—
>> With the first dream that comes with the
>>> first sleep
>> I run, I run, I am gathered to thy heart.

This is young poetry. Later she would gladly have withdrawn it, but her public and her husband would not have it so. Here was the only large and lasting dispute, I think, between my parents. My mother's view of poetry, in its heyday of Victorian grandiloquence, when there was a special poet's vocabulary, is told in a lovely later poem. In this Alice Meynell compares the similes, raptures, metaphors, the 'fair and flagrant things' of poetry, first to the simple inmost shrine of a great temple, and then to the Epiphany kings laden with gold

and frankincense and myrrh. The finest poetry,
she says, is at the journey's end:

> Plain, behind oracles, it is; and past
> All symbols, simple; perfect, heavenly-wild;
> The song some loaded poets reach at last—
> The kings that found a child.

Do you share my feeling that she herself here
reaches that inner simplicity?—

> The song some loaded poets reach at last—
> The kings that found a child.

And do you discover the artifice of the verse: not
forced on you but upholding the lines—the allitera-
tion of 'song' and 'some,' of 'loaded' and 'last'—
the heavy repeated vowel of *loaded* and *poet* . . .

I have said that Alice Meynell was the most
loved of women. She had the love of her husband
—my father, now ninety-five years old, still in this
year of her centenary celebration strongly alive in
all his faculties. She had the love of her family—
seven children who grew up in the most devoted
and familiar relationship: loving her as children
love a mother benevolent in all her thoughts, beneficent in all her actions; but, besides this private
relation with her, sharing with the world, though
at closer hand, her public attributes: her majesty,
her grace, her judgment, her fame and her poetry.
But this was far from all. She was loved too by
two great men of her day, both high poets—Coventry Patmore and Francis Thompson; loved hope-
lessly and magnificently; and, oddly, fantastically,
it was her great friendship with another writer,
George Meredith, which, they felt, hindered and
intercepted their own relation with her.

Coventry Patmore was almost an old man when
he met her. She had the most fervent love for his

poetry, he for her womanhood. What a strange closeness, what a hopeless incompatibility, was here! His personal love brought him within the nearest range that anyone could attain to her scrupulous life. The ordinary measure of closeness is acceptance: for them, it was denial. That was his distinction—he was allowed to come at least close enough for denial. Of her he had written:

> Her body, too, is so like her—
>   Sharp honey assuaged with milk,
> Straight as a stalk of lavender,
>   Soft as a rope of silk.

But this was her answer:

>   Why wilt thou chide,
> Who hast attained to be denied?
>   O learn, above
> All price is my refusal, Love.
>   My sacred Nay
> Was never cheapened by the way.
> Thy single sorrow crowns thee lord
> Of an unpurchasable word.
>
>   O strong, O pure!
> As Yea makes happier loves secure,
> I vow thee this
> Unique rejection of a kiss.
> I guard for thee
> This jealous sad monopoly.
> I seal this honour thine; none dare
> Hope for a part in thy despair.

But what made the tragedy of Patmore's later life was rather that neglect which must always seem to exist when of two people one concentrates

entirely on their personal relationship and the
other only in moments left over from other happy
absorptions. Fatal inequality! Without this love
she was whole; he was not. The same was true of
Francis Thompson. His love was almost an irrelev-
ance in her life. The fact that his great love poems
were addressed to her was a thing she never even
referred to, either to family or friend. She read
as literature, hardly as homage, the poems he wrote
to her even when they were as personal as this:

> How can I gauge what beauty is her dole
> Who cannot see her countenance for her soul . .

or

> Hers is the face whence all should copied be
> Did God make replicas of such as she.

To her Francis Thompson was a poet, and a child
—always a child, though he was but twelve years
younger. That is how she wrote to him "My dear
child" . . .

There were in fact three great relevancies in
Alice Meynell's life, leaving no voids craving to
be filled. Religion, literature and family—and she
was all lover for all these.

Her absorbing love of literature often made
literature itself her theme in verse. The fact that
Alice Meynell was alive before the tercentenary of
Shakespeare's birth in 1864, and after the tercentenary of his death in 1916, produced the poem in
which she makes her own years enclose the whole
of his briefer ones; so that she invokes him thus:

> O thou city of God
> My waste lies after thee, and lies before.

A like idea possessed her when she was about to

pass the age at which her father had died, in this
poem addressed to her father:

> Oh by my filial tears
> Mourned all too young, Father! On this my
>   head
> Time yet will force at last the longer years,
>   Claiming some strang respect for me from
>   you, the dead.
>
> Nay, nay! Too new to know
> Time's conjuring is, too great to understand.
> Memory has not died; it leaves me so—
>   Leaning a fading brow on your unfaded
>   hand.

And because it was her theme, how could I escape
an echo of her feeling when, quite lately, some
very early poems of hers which had never been
printed were discovered in a writing-book of hers
made when she was seventeen years old? From my
greater age I too saw, I newly met, my mother as
a young girl in those long-hidden lines.

But what kind of woman was she? Not all God-
dess, not all saint, not the very Muse surely. But
that is how most people saw her: that is how they
wrote of her. To her children as they became ado-
lescent she was someone to be protected—from
bores, from counting change, from finding her own
'bus routes; and to her husband—a writer in his
own right, but always willing to be her impressario
rather than his own—to her husband, someone to
be protected from her own rigid judgments and
prejudices. She had a number of these decisive
attitudes—that Gibbon had helped to corrupt the
English language with automatic phrases like:
"the brutal and licentious soldiery," or "flushed
with success." I think now she was over-protected,
even a little constrained with care. Our view of

her—the family view—was that she was complete—
completely just, holy, sure, happy, but how could
complete happiness write like this, in a poem called
"To Sleep?"

> Dear fool, be true to me!
> I know the poets speak thee fair, and I
> Hail thee uncivilly.
> O but I call with a more urgent cry!
>
> Come and release me; bring
> My irresponsible mind; come in thy hours;
> Draw from my soul the sting
> Of wit that trembles, consciousness that
> cowers.
>
> For if night comes without thee
> She is more cruel than day. But thou, fulfil
> Thy work thy gifts about thee—
> Liberty, liberty, from this weight of will.

This is human and heroic as well. But I remember—remember now with regret that I didn't
realize then, and so couldn't pander to them—her
unheroic little vanities; her hiding of her age, her
careful disguise too of the marks of that age, her
intense pleasure in praise, her serious dismay when
the household arrangements for dinner guests
went wrong and food, for example, was inadequate.
Can you be the mother of eight children and work
and work and work to house and feed and teach
them and not be human, And human, how spiritual-
ly human, is this passage from a letter, written in
her old age—but her mind was never old—to a nun
who was her confidant:

> "All my troubles are little, old, foolish, trivial
> as they always were—the troubles of my spiri-
> tual life, I mean. But as to sorrow, my failure
> of love to those that loved me can never be can-

celled or undone. So I never fail in a provision of grief for any night of my life.''

So she made atonement; so Patmore, so Francis Thompson, so her lovely and devoted American friend Agnes Tobin, received too late the tragic concentration of her attention in long years of wakeful and prayerful nights.

To be just to my father, as she was just; to be devoted to my father, as she was devoted, it is fitting that the last words of hers to be set down in this preface should be words which she wrote to him:

> Home, home from the horizon far and clear,
>   Hither the soft wings sweep;
> Flocks of the memories of the day draw near
>   The dovecote doors of sleep.
>
> Oh, which are they that come through sweetest light
>   Of all these homing birds?
> Which with the straightest and the swiftest flight?
>   Your words to me, your words!

Sir Francis Meynell.

WINDS AND WATERS

CERES' RUNAWAY

ONE can hardly be dull possessing the pleasant imaginary picture of a Municipality hot in chase of a wild crop—at least while the charming quarry escapes, as it does in Rome. The Municipality does not exist that would be nimble enough to overtake the Roman growth of green in the high places of the city. It is true that there have been the famous captures—those in the Colosseum, and in the Baths of Caracalla; moreover a less conspicuous running to earth takes place on the Appian Way, in some miles of the solitude of the Campagna, where men are employed in weeding the roadside. They slowly uproot the grass and lay it on the ancient stones—rows of little corpses —for sweeping up, as at Peckham; one wonders why. The governors of the city will not succeed in making the Via Appia look busy, or its stripped stones suggestive of a thriving commerce. Again, at the cemetery within the now torn and shattered Aurelian wall by the Porta San Paolo, they are often mowing of buttercups. "A light of laughing flowers along the grass is spread," says Shelley, whose child lies between Keats and the pyramid. But a couple of active scythes are kept at work there summer and spring—not that the grass is long, for it is much overtopped by the bee-orchis, but because flowers are not to laugh within reach of the civic vigilance.

3

Yet, except that it is overtaken and put to death in these accessible places, the wild summer growth of Rome has a prevailing success and victory. It breaks all bounds, flies to the summits, lodges in the sun, swings in the wind, takes wing to find the remotest ledges, and blooms aloft. It makes light of the sixteenth century, of the seventeenth, and of the eighteenth. As the historic ages grow cold it banters them alike. The flagrant flourishing statue, the haughty façade, the interrupted pediment (and Rome is chiefly the city of the interrupted pediment) are the opportunities of this vagrant garden in the air. One certain church, that is full of attitude, can hardly be aware that a crimson snap-dragon of great stature and many stalks and blossoms is standing on its furthest summit tiptoe against its sky. The cornice of another church in the fair middle of Rome lifts out of the shadows of the streets a row of acci-dental marigolds. Impartial to the antique, the mediaeval, the Renaissance early and late, the newer modern, this wild summer finds its account in travertine and tufa, reticulated work, brick, stucco, and stone. "A bird of the air carries the matter," or the last sea-wind, sombre and soft, or the latest tramontana, gold and blue, has lodged in a little fertile dust the wild grass, wild wheat, wild oats!

If Venus had her runaway, after whom the Eliza-bethans raised hue and cry, this is Ceres'. The muni-cipal authorities, hot-foot, cannot catch it. And, worse than all, if they pause, dismayed, to mark the flight of the agile fugitive safe on the arc of a flying buttress, or taking the place of the fallen mosaics and coloured tiles of a twelfth-century tower, and in any case inaccessible, the grass grows under their discomfited feet. It actually casts a flush of green over their city *piazza*—the wide light-gray pavements so vast that to keep them weeded would need an army of workers. That army has not been employed; and grass grows in a small way, but still beautifully, in the wide space around which the tramway circles. Perhaps a hatred of its delightful presence is what chiefly prompts the civic government in Rome to the effort to turn the *piazza* into a square. The shrub is to take the place not so much of the pavement as of the importunate grass. For it is hard to be beaten—and the weed does so prevail, is so small, and so dominant! The sun takes its part, and one might almost imagine a sensitive Municipality in tears, to see grass running, overhead and underfoot, through the "third" (which is in truth the fourth) Rome. Piranesi, all-romantic, on the other hand, loves the runaway so well that he nourishes it. It grows ostensibly wild, in his beautiful engravings, with a kind of luxury. He makes it, too, a Romantic.

When I say grass I use the word widely. Italian grass is not turf; it is full of things, and they are chiefly aromatic. No richer scents throng each other, close and warm, than these from a little hand-space of the grass one rests on, within the walls or on the plain, or in the Sabine or the Alban hills. Moreover, under the name I will take leave to include lettuce as it grows with a most welcome surprise on certain ledges of the Vatican. That great and beautiful palace is piled, at various angles, as it were house upon house, here magnificent, here careless, but with nothing pretentious and nothing furtive. And outside one lateral

window on a ledge to the sun, prospers this little
garden of random salad. Buckingham Palace has
nothing whatever of the Vatican dignity, but one cannot well think of little cheerful cabbages sunning themselves on any parapet it may have round a corner.

Moreover, in Italy the vegetables—the table ones—
have a wildness, a suggestion of the grass, from lands
at liberty, for all the tilling. Wildish peas, wilder asparagus—the field asparagus which seems to have disappeared from England, but of which Herrick boasts
in his manifestations of frugality—and strawberries
much less than half-way from the small and darkling
ones of the woods to the pale and corpulent of the
gardens, and with nothing of the wild fragrance lost—
these are all Italian things of savage savour and simplicity. The most cultivated of all countries, the Italy
of tillage, is yet not a garden, but something better, as
her city is yet not a town but something better, and
her wilderness something better than a desert. In all
the three there is a trace of the little flying heels of the
runaway.

WELLS

THE world at present is inclined to make sorry mysteries or unattractive secrets of the methods and supplies of the fresh and perennial means of life. A very dull secret is made of water, for example, and the plumber sets his seal upon the floods whereby we live. They are covered, they are carried, they are hushed, from the spring to the tap; and when their voices are released at last in the London scullery, why, it can hardly be said that the song is eloquent of the natural source of waters, whether earthly or heavenly. There is not one of the circumstances of this capture of streams—the company, the water-rate, and the rest —that is not a sign of the ill-luck of modern devices in regard to style. For style implies a candour and simplicity of means, an action, a gesture, as it were, in the doing of small things; it is the ignorance of secret ways; whereas the finish of modern life and its neatness seem to be secured by a system of little shufflings and surprises.

Dress, among other things, is furnished throughout with such fittings; they form its very construction. Style does not exist in modern arrayings, for all their prettiness and precision, and for all the successes— which are not to be denied—of their outer part; the happy little swagger that simulates style is but another sign of its absence, being prepared by mere dodges and dexterities beneath, and the triumph and success of the present art of raiment—" fit " itself—is but the result of a masked and lurking labour and device.

The masters of fine manners, moreover, seem to be always aware of the beauty that comes of pausing slightly upon the smaller and slighter actions, such as meaner men are apt to hurry out of the way. In a word, the workman, with his finish and accomplishment, is the dexterous provider of contemporary things; and the ready, well-appointed, and decorated life of all towns is now altogether in his hands; whereas the artist craftsman of other times made a manifestation of his means. The first hides the streams, under stress and pressure, in paltry pipes which we all must make haste to call upon the earth to cover, and the second lifted up the arches of the aqueduct.

The search of easy ways to live is not always or everywhere the way to ugliness, but in some countries, at some dates, it is the sure way. In all countries, and at all dates, extreme finish compassed by hidden means must needs, from the beginning, prepare the abolition of dignity. This is easy to understand, but it is less easy to explain the ill-fortune that presses upon the expert workman, in search of easy ways to live, all the ill-favoured materials, makes them cheap for him, makes them serviceable and effectual, urges him to use them, seal them, and inter them, turning the trim and dull completeness out to the view of the daily world. It is an added mischance. Nor, on the other hand, is it easy to explain the beautiful good luck attending the simpler devices which are, after all, only less expert ways of labour. In those happy conditions, neither from the material, suggesting to the workman, nor from the workman looking askance at his unhandsome material, comes a first proposal to pour in cement and make fast the underworld, out of sight. But fate spares not that suggestion to the able and the unlucky at their task of making neat work of the means, the distribution, the traffic of life.

The springs, then, the profound wells, the streams, are of all the means of our lives those which we should wish to see open to the sun, with their waters on their progress and their way to us; but, no, they are lapped in lead.

King Pandion and his friends lie not under heavier seals.

> King Pandion he is dead,
> All his friends are lapped in lead.

Yet we have been delighted, elsewhere, by open floods. The hiding-place that nature and the simpler crafts allot to the waters of wells are, at their deepest, in communication with the open sky. No other mine is so visited; for the noonday sun himself is visible there; and it is fine to think of the waters of this planet, shallow and profound, all charged with shining suns, a multitude of waters multiplying suns, and carrying that remote fire, as it were, within their unalterable freshness. Not a pool without this visitant, or without passages of stars. As for the wells of the Equator, you may think of them in their last recesses as the daily bathing-places of light; a luminous fancy is able so to scatter fitful figures of the sun, and to plunge them in thousands within those deeps.

Round images lie in the dark waters, but in the
bright waters the sun is shattered out of its circle,
scattered into waves, broken across stones, and rippled
over sand; and in the shallow rivers that fall through
chestnut woods the image is mingled with the mobile
figures of leaves. To all these waters the agile air has
perpetual access. Not so can great towns be watered, it
will be said with reason; and this is precisely the ill-
luck of great towns.

Nevertheless, there are towns, not, in a sense, so
great, that have the grace of visible wells; such as
Venice, where the *campo* has its circle of carved stone,
its clashing of dark copper on the pavement, its soft
kiss of the copper vessel with the surface of the water
below, and the cheerful work of the cable.

Or the Romans knew how to cause the parted
floods to measure their plain with the strong, steady,
and level flight of arches from the watersheds in the
hills to the arid city; and having the waters captive,
they knew how to compel them to take part, by
fountains, in this Roman triumph. They had the wit
to boast thus of their brilliant prisoner.

None more splendid came bound to Rome, or graced
captivity with a more invincible liberty of the heart.
And the captivity and the leap of the heart of the waters
have outlived their captors. They have remained in
Rome, and have remained alone. Over them the victory
was longer than empire, and their thousands of loud
voices have never ceased to confess the conquest of the
cold floods, separated long ago, drawn one by one, alive,
to the head and front of the world.

Of such a transit is made no secret. It was the

most manifest fact of Rome. You could not look to
the city from the mountains or to the distance from
the city without seeing the approach of those perpetual
waters—waters bound upon daily tasks and minute
services. This, then, was the style of a master, who
does not lapse from "incidental greatness," has no
mean precision, out of sight, to prepare the finish of
his phrases, and does not think the means and the
approaches are to be plotted and concealed. Without
anxiety, without haste, and without misgiving are all
great things to be done, and neither interruption in the
doing nor ruin after they are done finds anything in
them to betray. There was never any disgrace of
means, and when the world sees the work broken
through there is no disgrace of discovery. The labour
of Michelangelo's chisel, little more than begun, a
Roman structure long exposed in disarray—upon these
the light of day looks full, and the Roman and the
Florentine have their unrefuted praise.

RAIN

NOT excepting the falling stars—for they are far less sudden—there is nothing in nature that so outstrips our unready eyes as the familiar rain. The rods that thinly stripe our landscape, long shafts from the clouds, if we had but agility to make the arrowy downward journey with them by the glancing of our eyes, would be infinitely separate, units, an innumerable flight of single things, and the simple movement of intricate points.

The long stroke of the raindrop, which is the drop and its path at once, being our impression of a shower, shows us how certainly our impression is the effect of the lagging, and not of the haste, of our senses. What we are apt to call our quick impression is rather our sensibly tardy, unprepared, surprised, outrun, lightly bewildered sense of things that flash and fall, wink, and are overpast and renewed, while the gentle eyes of man hesitate and mingle the beginning with the close. These inexpert eyes, delicately baffled, detain for an instant the image that puzzles them, and so dally with the bright progress of a meteor, and part slowly from the slender course of the already fallen raindrop, whose moments are not theirs. There seems to be such a difference of instants as invests all swift movement with mystery in man's eyes, and causes the past, a moment old, to be written, vanishing, upon the skies.

The visible world is etched and engraved with the signs and records of our halting apprehension; and the pause between the distant woodman's stroke with the axe and its sound upon our ears is repeated in the impressions of our clinging sight. The round wheel dazzles it, and the stroke of the bird's wing shakes it off like a captivity evaded. Everywhere the natural haste is impatient of these timid senses; and their perception, outrun by the shower, shaken by the light, denied by the shadow, eluded by the distance, makes the lingering picture that is all our art. One of the most constant causes of all the mystery and beauty of that art is surely not that we see by flashes, but that nature flashes on our meditative eyes. There is no need for the impressionist to make haste, nor would haste avail him, for mobile nature doubles upon him, and plays with his delays the exquisite game of visibility.

Momently visible in a shower, invisible within the earth, the ministration of water is so manifest in the coming rain-cloud that the husbandman is allowed to see the rain of his own land, yet unclaimed in the arms of the rainy wind. It is an eager lien that he binds the shower withal, and the grasp of his anxiety is on the coming cloud. His sense of property takes aim and reckons distance and speed, and even as he shoots a little ahead of the equally uncertain ground-game, he knows approximately how to hit the cloud of his possession. So much is the rain bound to the earth that, unable to compel it, man has yet found a way, by lying in wait, to put his price upon it. The exhaustible cloud "outweeps its rain," and only the inexhaustible sun seems to repeat and to enforce his cumulative fires upon every span of ground, innumerable.

Baby of the cloud, rain is carried long enough within that troubled breast to make all the multitude of days unlike each other. Rain, as the end of the cloud, divides light and withholds it; in its flight warning away the sun, and in its final fall dismissing shadow. It is a threat and a reconciliation; it removes mountains compared with which the Alps are hillocks, and makes a childlike peace between opposed heights and battlements of heaven.

THE TOW PATH

A CHILDISH pleasure in producing small mechanical effects unaided must have some part in
the sense of enterprise wherewith you gird your
shoulders with the tackle, and set out, alone but
necessary, on the even path of the lopped and grassy
side of the Thames—the side of meadows.

The elastic resistance of the line is a "heart-ani-
mating strain," only too slight; and sensible is the
thrill in it as the ranks of the riverside plants, with
their small summit-flower of violet-pink, are swept
aside like a long green breaker of flourishing green.
The line drums lightly in the ears when the bushes are
high and it grows taut; it makes a telephone for the
rush of flowers under the stress of your easy power.

The active delights of one who is not athletic are
few, like the joys of "'feeling hearts" according to the
erroneous sentiment of a verse of Moore's. The joys of
sensitive hearts are many; but the joys of sensitive
hands are few. Here, however, in the effectual act of
towing, is the ample revenge of the unmuscular upon
the happy labourers with the oar, the pole, the bicycle,
and all other means of violence. Here, on the long
tow-path, between warm, embrowned meadows and
opal waters, you need but to walk in your swinging
harness, and so take your friends up-stream.

You work merely as the mill-stream works—by

simple movement. At lock after lock along a hundred miles, deep-roofed mills shake to the wheel that turns by no greater stress, and you and the river have the same mere force of progress. There never was any kinder incentive of companionship. It is the bright Thames walking softly in your blood, or you that are flowing by so many curves of low shore on the level of the world.

The birds, flying high for mountain air in the heat, wing nothing but their own weight. You will not envy them for so brief a success. Did not Wordsworth want a "little boat" for the air? Did not Byron call him a blockhead therefor? Wordsworth had, perhaps, a sense of towing.

All the advantage of the expert is nothing in this simple industry. Even the athlete, though he may go further, cannot do better than you, walking your effectual walk with the line attached to your willing steps. Your moderate strength of a mere everyday physical education gives you the sufficient mastery of the tow path. If your natural walk is heavy, there is spirit in the tackle to give it life, and if it is buoyant it will be more buoyant under the buoyant burden—the yielding check—than ever before. An unharnessed walk must begin to seem to you a sorry incident of insignificant liberty. It is easier than towing? So is the drawing of water in a sieve easier to the arms than drawing in a bucket, but not to the heart. To walk unbound is to walk in prose, without the friction of the wings of metre, without the sweet and encouraging tug upon the spirit and the line.

No dead weight follows you as you tow   The burden

is willing; it depends upon you gaily, as a friend may do without making any depressing show of helplessness; neither, on the other hand, is it apt to set you at naught or charge you with a make-believe. It accompanies, it almost anticipates; it lags when you are brisk, just so much as to give your briskness good reason, and to justify you if you should take to still more nimble heels. All your haste, moreover, does but waken a more brilliantly-sounding ripple.

The bounding and rebounding burden you carry (but it nearly seems to carry you, so fine is the mutual good will) gives work to your figure, enlists your erect-ness and your gait, but leaves your eyes free. No watch-ing of mechanisms for the labourer of the tow-path. What little outlook is to be kept falls to the lot of the steerer smoothly towed. Your easy and efficient work lets you carry your head high and watch the birds, or listen to them. They fly in such lofty air that they seem to turn blue in the blue sky. A flash of their flight shows silver for a moment, but they are blue birds in that sunny distance above, as mountains are blue, and horizons. The days are so still that you do not merely hear the cawing of the rooks—you overhear their hundred private croakings and creak-ings, the soliloquy of the solitary places swept by wings.

As for songs, it is September, and the silence of July is long at an end. This year's robins are in full voice; and the only song that is not for love or nesting—the childish song of boy-birds, the freshest and youngest note—is, by a happy paradox, that of an autumnal voice.

Here is no hoot, nor hurry of engines, nor whisper of the cyclist's wheel, nor foot upon a road, to overcome that light but resounding note. Silent are feet on the grassy brink, like the innocent, stealthy soles of the barefooted in the south.

THE TETHERED CONSTELLATIONS

I T is no small thing—no light discovery—to find a river Andromeda and Arcturus and their bright neighbours wheeling for half a summer night on their way around a pole-star in the waters. One star or two—delicate visitants of streams—we are used to see, somewhat by a sleight of the eyes, so fine and so fleeting is that apparition. Or the southern waves may show the light—not the image—of the evening or the morning planet. But this, in a pool of the country Thames at night, is no ripple-lengthened light; it is the startling image of a whole large constellation burning in the flood.

These reflected heavens are different heavens. On a darker and more vacant field than that of the real skies, the shape of the Lyre or the Bear has an altogether new and noble solitude; and the waters play a painter's part in setting their splendid subject free. Two movements shake but do not scatter the still night: the bright flashing of constellations in the deep Weir-pool, and the dark flashes of the vague bats flying. The stars in the stream fluctuate with an alien motion. Reversed, estranged, isolated, every shape of large stars escapes and returns, escapes and returns. Fitful in the steady night, those constellations, so few, so whole, and so remote, have a suddenness of gleaming life. You imagine that some unexampled gale might make them seem to shine with such a movement in the veritable sky; yet nothing but deep water, seeming still in its incessant flight and rebound, could really show such altered stars. The flood lets a constellation fly, as Juliet's "wanton" with a tethered bird, only to pluck it home again. At moments some rhythmic flux of the water seems about to leave the darkly-set, widely-spaced Bear absolutely at large, to dismiss the great stars, and refuse to imitate the skies, and all the water is obscure; then one broken star returns, then fragments of another, and a third and a fourth flit back to their noble places, brilliantly vague, wonderfully visible, mobile, and unalterable. There is nothing else at once so keen and so elusive.

The aspen poplar had been in captive flight all day, but with no such vanishings as these. The dimmer constellations of the soft night are reserved by the skies. Hardly is a secondary star seen by the large and vague eyes of the stream. They are blind to the Pleiades.

There is a little kind of star that drowns itself by hundreds in the river Thames—the many-rayed silver-white seed that makes journeys on all the winds up and down England and across it in the end of summer. It is a most expert traveller, turning a little wheel a-tiptoe wherever the wind lets it rest, and speeding on those pretty points when it is not flying. The streets of London are among its many highways, for it is fragile enough to go far in all sorts of weather. But it gets disabled if a rough gust tumbles it on the water so that its finely-feathered feet are wet. On gentle breezes it is able to cross dry-shod, walking the waters.

All unlike is this pilgrim star to the tethered constellations. It is far adrift. It goes singly to all the winds. It offers thistle plants (or whatever is the flower that makes such delicate ashes) to the tops of many thousand hills. Doubtless the farmer would rather have to meet it in battalions than in these invincible units astray. But if the farmer owes it a lawful grudge, there is many a rigid riverside garden wherein it would give me great pleasure to sow the thistles of the nearest pasture.

RUSHES AND REEDS

TALLER than the grass and lower than the trees, there is another growth that feels the implicit spring. It had been more abandoned to winter than even the short grass shuddering under a wave of east wind, more than the dumb trees. For the multitudes of sedges, rushes, canes, and reeds were the appropriate lyre of the cold. On them the keen winds played their dry music. They were part of the winter. It looked through them and spoke through them. They were spears and javelins in array to the sound of the drums of the north.

The winter takes fuller possession of these things than of those that stand solid. The sedges whistle his tune. They let the colour of his light look through—low-flying arrows and bright bayonets of winter day.

The multitudes of all reeds and rushes grow out of bounds. They belong to the margins of lands, the space between the farms and the river, beyond the pastures, and where the marsh in flower becomes perilous footing for the cattle. They are the fringe of the low lands, the sign of streams. They grow tall between you and the near horizon of flat lands. They etch their sharp lines upon the sky; and near them grow flowers of stature, including the lofty yellow lily.

Our green country is the better for the gray, soft, cloudy darkness of the sedge, and our full landscape is the better for the distinction of its points, its needles, and its resolute right lines.

Ours is a summer full of voices, and therefore it does not so need the sound of rushes; but they are most sensitive to the stealthy breezes, and betray the passing of a wind that even the tree-tops knew not of. Sometimes it is a breeze unfelt, but the stiff sedges whisper it along a mile of marsh. To the strong wind they bend, showing the silver of their sombre little tassels as fish show the silver of their sides turning in the pathless sea. They are unanimous. A field of tall flowers tosses many ways in one warm gale, like the many lovers of a poet who have a thousand reasons for their love; but the rushes, more strongly tethered, are swept into a single attitude, again and again, at every renewal of the storm.

Between the pasture and the wave, the many miles of rushes and reeds in England seem to escape that insistent ownership which has so changed (except for a few forests and downs) the aspect of England, and has in fact made the landscape. Cultivation makes the landscape elsewhere, rather than ownership, for the boundaries in the south are not conspicuous; but here it is ownership. But the rushes are a gipsy people, amongst us, yet out of reach. The landowner, if he is rather a gross man, believes these races of reeds are his. But if he is a man of sensibility, depend upon it he has his interior doubts. His property, he says, goes right down to the centre of the earth, in the shape of a wedge; how high up it goes into the air it would be difficult to say, and obviously the shape of the wedge must be continued in the direction of increase. We may therefore proclaim his right to the clouds and their cargo. It is true that as his ground game is apt to go upon his neighbour's land to be shot, so the clouds may now and then spend his showers elsewhere. But the great thing is the view. A well-appointed country-house sees nothing out of the windows that is not its own. But he who tells you so, and proves it to you by his own view, is certainly disturbed by an unspoken doubt, if his otherwise contented eyes should happen to be caught by a region of rushes. The water is his—he had the pond made; or the river, for a space, and the fish, for a time. But the bulrushes, the reeds! One wonders whether a very thorough landowner, but a sensitive one, ever resolved that he would endure this sort of thing no longer, and went out armed and had a long acre of sedges scythed to death.

They are probably outlaws. They are dwellers upon thresholds and upon margins, as the gipsies make a home upon the green edges of a road. No wild flowers, however wild, are rebels. The copses and their prim-roses are good subjects, the oaks are loyal. Now and then, though, one has a kind of suspicion of some of the other kinds of trees—the Corot trees. Standing at a distance from the more ornamental trees, from those of fuller foliage, and from all the indeciduous shrubs and the conifers (manifest property, every one), two or three translucent aspens, with which the very sun and the breath of earth are entangled, have sometimes seemed to wear a certain look—an extra-territorial look, let us call it. They are suspect. One is inclined to shake a doubtful head at them.

And the landowner feels it. He knows quite well,

though he may not say so, that the Corot trees, though
they do not dwell upon margins, are in spirit almost as
extra-territorial as the rushes. In proof of this he very
often cuts them down, out of the view, once for all.
The view is better, as a view, without them. Though
their roots are in his ground right enough, there is
a something about their heads——. But the
reason he gives for wishing them away
is merely that they are " thin."
A man does not always
say everything.

IN A BOOK ROOM

A NORTHERN FANCY

"I REMEMBER," said Dryden, writing to Dennis, "I remember poor Nat Lee, who was then upon the verge of madness, yet made a sober and witty answer to a bad poet who told him, 'It was an easy thing to write like a madman.' 'No,' said he, ''tis a very difficult thing to write like a madman, but 'tis a very easy thing to write like a fool.'" Nevertheless, the difficult song of distraction is to be heard, a light high note, in English poetry throughout two centuries at least, and one English poet lately set that untethered lyric, the mad maid's song, flying again.

A revolt against the oppression of the late sixteenth and early seventeenth centuries—the age of the rediscovery of death; against the crime of tragedies; against the tyranny of Italian example that had made the poets walk in one way of love, scorn, constancy, inconstancy—such a revolt may have caused this trolling of unconsciousness, this tune of innocence, and this carol of liberty, to be held so dear. "I heard a maid in Bedlam," runs the old song. High and low the poets tried for that note, and the singer was nearly always to be a maid and crazed for love. Except for the temporary insanity so indifferently worn by the soprano of the now deceased kind of Italian opera, and except that a recent French story plays with the flitting figure of a village girl robbed of her wits by woe (and this, too, is

29

a Russian villager, and the Southern author may have found his story on the spot, as he seems to aver) I have not met elsewhere than in England this solitary and detached poetry of the treble note astray.

At least, it is principally a northern fancy. Would the steadfast Cordelia, if she had not died, have lifted the low voice to that high note, so delicately untuned? She who would not be prodigal of words might yet, indeed, have sung in the cage, and told old tales, and laughed at gilded butterflies of the court of crimes, and lived so long in the strange health of an emancipated brain as to wear out

> Packs and sects of great ones
> That ebb and flow by the moon.

She, if King Lear had had his last desire, might have sung the merry and strange tune of Bedlam, like the slighter Ophelia and the maid called Barbara.

It was surely the name of the maid who died singing, as Desdemona remembers, that lingered in the ear of Wordsworth. Of all the songs of the distracted, written in the sanity of high imagination, there is nothing more passionate than that beginning " 'Tis said that some have died for love." To one who has always recognized the greatness of this poem and who possibly had known and forgotten how much Ruskin prized it, it was a pleasure to find the judgement afresh in *Modern Painters*, where this grave lyric is cited for an example of great imagination. It is the mourning and restless song of the lover ("the pretty Barbara died") who has not yet broken free from memory into the alien world of the insane.

Barbara's lover dwelt in the scene of his love, as Dryden's Adam entreats the expelling angel that he might do, protesting that he could endure to lose "the bliss, but not the place." (And although this dramatic "Paradise Lost" of Dryden's is hardly named by critics except to be scorned, this is assuredly a fine and imaginative thought.) It is nevertheless as a wanderer that the crazed creature visits the fancy of English poets with such a wild recurrence. The Englishman of the far past, barred by climate, bad roads, ill-lighted winters, and the intricate life and customs of the little town, must have been generally a home-keeper. No adventure, no setting forth, and small liberty, for him. But Tom-a-Bedlam, the wild man in patches or in ribbons, with his wallet and his horn for alms of food or drink, came and went as fitfully as the storm, free to suffer all the cold—an unsheltered creature; and the chill fancy of the villager followed him out to the heath on a journey that had no law. Was it he in person, or a poet for him, that made the swinging song: "From the hag and the hungry goblin"? If a poet, it was one who wrote like a madman and not like a fool.

Not a town, not a village, not a solitary cottage during the English Middle Ages was unvisited by him who frightened the children; they had a name for him as for the wild birds—Robin Redbreast, Dicky Swallow, Philip Sparrow, Tom Tit, Tom-a-Bedlam. And after him came the "Abram men," who were sane parodies of the crazed, and went to the fairs and wakes in motley. Evelyn says of a fop: "All his body was dressed like a maypole, or a Tom-a-Bedlam's cap." But after the Civil Wars they vanished, and no man knew how. In time old men remembered them only to remember that they had not seen any such companies or solitary wanderers of late years.

The mad maid of the poets is a vagrant too, when she is free, and not singing within Bedlam early in the morning, "in the spring." Wordsworth, who dealt with the legendary fancy in his "Ruth," makes the crazed one a wanderer in the hills whom a traveller might see by chance, rare as an Oread, and nearly as wild as Echo herself:

> I too have passed her in the hills
> Setting her little water-mills.

His heart misgives him to think of the rheumatism that must befall in such a way of living; and his grave sense of civilization, *bourgeois* in the humane and noble way that is his own, restores her after death to the company of man, to the "holy bell," which Shakespeare's Duke remembered in banishment, and to the congregation and their "Christian psalm."

The older poets were less responsible, less serious and more sad, than Wordsworth, when they in turn were touched by the fancy of the maid crazed by love. They left her to her light immortality; and she might be drenched in dews; they would not desire to reconcile nor bury her. She might have her hair torn by the bramble, but her heart was light after trouble. "Many light hearts and wings"—she had at least the bird's heart, and the poet lent to her voice the wings of his verses.

There is nothing in our poetry less modern than she. The vagrant woman of later feeling was rather the sane creature of Ebenezer Elliott's fine lines in "The Excursion "—

> Bone-weary, many-childed, trouble-tried!
> Wife of my bosom, wedded to my soul!

Trouble did not "try" the Elizabethan wild one, it undid her. She had no child, or if there had ever been a child of hers, she had long forgotten how it died. She hailed the wayfarer, who was more weary than she, with a song; she haunted the cheerful dawn; her "good-morrow" rings from Herrick's poem, fresh as cock-crow. She knows that her love is dead, and her perplexity has regard rather to the many kinds of flowers than to the old story of his death; they distract her in the splendid meadows.

All the tragic world paused to hear that lightest of songs, as the tragedy of *Hamlet* pauses for the fitful voice of Ophelia. Strange was the charm of this perpetual alien, and unknown to us now. The world has become once again as it was in the mad maid's heyday, less serious and more sad than Wordsworth; but it has not recovered, and perhaps will never recover, that sweetness. Blake's was a more starry madness. Crabbe, writing of village sorrows, thought himself bound to recur to the legend of the mad maid, but his "crazed maiden" is sane enough, sorrowful but dull, and sings of her own "burning brow," as Herrick's wild one never sang; nor is there any smile in her story, though she talks of flowers, or, rather, "the herbs I loved to rear"; and perhaps she is the surest of all signs that the strange inspiration of the past centuries was lost, vanished like Tom-a-Bedlam himself. It had been wholly English, whereas the English eighteenth century was not wholly English.

It is not to be imagined that the hard Southern mind could ever have played in poetry with such a fancy; or that Petrarch, for example, could so have forgone the manifestation of intelligence and intelligible sentiment. And as to Dante, who put the two eternities into the momentary balance of the human will, cold would be his disregard of this northern dream of innocence. If the mad maid was an alien upon earth, what were she in the Inferno? What word can express her strangeness there, her vagrancy there? And with what eyes would they see this dewy face glancing in at the windows of that City?

PATHOS

A FUGITIVE writer wrote not long ago on the fugitive page of a magazine: "For our part, the drunken tinker [Christopher Sly] is the most real personage of the piece, and not without some hints of the pathos that is worked out more fully, though by different ways, in Bottom and Malvolio." Has it indeed come to this? Have the Zeitgeist and the Weltschmerz or their yet later equivalents, compared with which "le spleen" of the French Byronic age was gay, done so much for us? Is there to be no laughter left in literature free from the preoccupation of a sham real-life? So it would seem. Even what the great master has not shown us in his work, that your critic convinced of pathos is resolved to see in it. By the penetration of his intrusive sympathy he will come at it. It is of little use now to explain Snug the joiner to the audience: why, it is precisely Snug who stirs their emotions so painfully. Not the lion; they can make shift to see through that: but the Snug within, the human Snug. And Master Shallow has the Weltschmerz in that latent form which is the more appealing; and discouraging questions arise as to the end of old Double; and Harpagon is the tragic figure of Monomania; and as to Argan, ah, what havoc in "les entrailles de Monsieur" must have been wrought by those prescriptions! *Et patati, et patata.*

35

It may be only too true that the actual world is "with pathos delicately edged." For Malvolio living we should have had living sympathies; so much aspiration, so ill-educated a love of refinement; so unarmed a credulity, noblest of weaknesses, betrayed for the laughter of a chambermaid. By an actual Bottom the weaver our pity might be reached for the sake of his single self-reliance, his fancy and resource condemned to burlesque and ignominy by the niggard doom of circumstance. But is not life one thing and is not art another? Is it not the privilege of literature to treat things singly, without the after-thoughts of life, without the troublous completeness of the many-sided world? Is not Shakespeare, for this reason, our refuge? Fortunately unreal is his world when he will have it so; and there we may laugh with open heart at a grotesque man: without misgiving, without remorse, without reluctance. If great creating Nature has not assumed for herself she has assuredly secured to the great creating poet the right of partiality, of limitation, of setting aside and leaving out, of taking one impression and one emotion as sufficient for the day. Art and Nature are complementary; in relation, not in confusion, with one another. And all this officious cleverness in seeing round the corner, as it were, of a thing presented by literary art in the flat—(the borrowing of similes from other arts is of evil tendency; but let this pass, as it is apt)—is but another sign of the general lack of a sense of the separation between Nature and her sentient mirror in the mind. In some of his persons, indeed, Shakespeare is as Nature herself, all-inclusive; but in others—and chiefly in comedy—he is partial, he is impressionary, he refuses to know what is not to his purpose, he is lightheartedly capricious. And in that gay, wilful world it is that he gives us—or used to give us, for even the word is obsolete—the pleasure of *oubliance*.

Now this fugitive writer has not been so swift but that I have caught him a clout as he went. Yet he will do it again; and those like-minded will assuredly also continue to show how much more completely human, how much more sensitive, how much more responsible, is the art of the critic than the world has ever dreamt till now. And, superior in so much, they will still count their importunate sensibility as the choicest of their gifts. And Lepidus, who loves to wonder, can have no better subject for his admiration than the pathos of the time. It is bred now of your mud by the operation of your sun. 'Tis a strange serpent; and the tears of it are wet.

ANIMA PELLEGRINA!

EVERY language in the world has its own phrase, fresh for the stranger's fresh and alien sense of its signal significance; a phrase that is its own essential possession, and yet is dearer to the speaker of other tongues. Easily—shall I say cheaply?—spiritual, for example, was the nation that devised the name *anima pellegrina*, wherewith to crown a creature admired. "Pilgrim soul" is a phrase for any language, but "pilgrim soul!" addressed, singly and sweetly, to one who cannot be overpraised, "pilgrim-soul!" is a phrase of fondness, the high homage of a lover, of one watching, of one who has no more need of common flatteries, but has admired and gazed while the object of his praises visibly surpassed them—this is the facile Italian ecstasy, and it rises into an Italian heaven.

It was by chance, and in an old play, that I came upon this impetuous, sudden, and single sentence of admiration, as it were a sentence of life passed upon one charged with inestimable deeds; and the modern editor had thought it necessary to explain the exclamation by a note. It was, he said, poetical.

Anima pellegrina seems to be Italian of no later date than Pergolese's airs, and suits the time as the familiar phrase of the more modern love-song suited the day of Bellini. But it is only Italian, bygone Italian, and not a part of the sweet past of any other European nation, but only of this.

38

To the same local boundaries and enclosed skies belongs the charm of those buoyant words:

Felice chi vi mira,
Ma più felice chi per voi sospira!

And it is not only a charm of elastic sound or of grace; that would be but a property of the turn of speech. It is rather the profounder advantage whereby the rhymes are freighted with such feeling as the very language keeps in store. In another tongue you may sing, "happy who looks, happier who sighs"; but in what other tongue shall the little meaning be so sufficient, and in what other shall you get from so weak an antithesis the illusion of a lovely intellectual epigram? Yet it is not worthy of an English reader to call it an illusion; he should rather be glad to travel into the place of a language where the phrase *is* intellectual, impassioned, and an epigram; and should thankfully for the occasion translate himself, and not the poetry.

I have been delighted to use a present current phrase whereof the charm may still be unknown to Englishmen—"*piuttosto bruttini*." See what an all-Italian spirit is here, and what contempt, not reluctant, but tolerant and familiar. You may hear it said of pictures, or works of art of several kinds, and you confess at once that not otherwise should they be condemned. *Brutto*—ugly—is the word of justice, the word for any language, everywhere translatable, a circular note, to be exchanged internationally with a general meaning, wholesale, in the course of the European concert. But *bruttino* is a soothing diminutive, a diminutive that forbears to express contempt, a diminutive that implies innocence, and is, moreover, guarded by a hesitating adverb, shrugging in the rear—"rather than not." "Rather ugly than not, and ugly in a little way that we need say few words about—the fewer the better"; nay, this paraphrase cannot achieve the homely Italian quality whereby the printed and condemnatory criticism is made a family affair that shall go no further. After the sound of it, the European concert seems to be composed of brass instruments.

How unlike is the house of English language and the·enclosure into which a traveller hither has to enter! Do we possess anything here more essentially ours (though we share it with our sister Germany) than our particle "un"? Poor are those living languages that have not our use of so rich a negative. The French equivalent in adjectives reaches no further than the adjective itself—or hardly; it does not attain the participle; so that no French or Italian poet has the words "unloved," "unforgiven." None such, therefore, has the opportunity of the gravest and the most majestic of all ironies. In our English, the words that are denied are still there—"loved," "forgiven": excluded angels, who stand erect, attesting what is not done, what is undone, what shall not be done.

No merely opposite words could have so much denial, or so much pain of loss, or so much outer darkness, or so much barred beatitude in sight. All-present, all-significant, all-remembering, all-foretelling is the word, and it has a plenitude of knowledge.

We have many more conspicuous possessions that are, like this, proper to character and thought, and by no means only an accident of untransferable speech. And it is impossible for a reader, who is a lover of languages for their spirit, to pass the words of untravelled excellence, proper to their own garden enclosed, without recognition. Never may they be disregarded or confounded with the universal stock. If I would not so neglect *piuttosto bruttini*, how much less a word dominating literature! And of such words of ascendancy and race there is no great English author but has abundant possession. No need to recall them. But even writers who are not great have, here and there, proved their full consciousness of their birthright. Thus does a man who was hardly an author, Haydon the painter, put out his hand to take his rights. He has incomparable language when he is at a certain page of his life; at that time he sate down to sketch his child, dying in its babyhood, and the head he studied was, he says, full of " power and grief."

This is a phrase of different discovery from that which reveals a local rhyme-balanced epigram, a gracious antithesis, taking an intellectual place—*Felice chi vi mira*—or the art-critic's phrase—*piuttosto bruttini*—of easy, companionable, and equal contempt.

As for French, if it had no other sacred words—and it has many—who would not treasure the language that has given us—no, not that has given us, but that has kept for its own—*ensoleillé*? Nowhere else is the sun served with such a word It is not to be said or written without a convincing sense of sunshine, and from the very word come light and radiation. The unaccustomed North could not have made it, nor the accustomed South, but only a nation part-north and

part-south; therefore neither England nor Italy can
rival it. But there needed also the senses of the French
—those senses of which they say far too much in every
second-class book of their enormous, their general
second-class, but which they have matched in their
time with some inimitable words. Perhaps that match-
ing was done at the moment of the full literary consciousness of the senses, somewhere about the famous
1830. For I do not think *ensoleillé* to be a much older
word—I make no assertion. Whatever its origin, may
it have no end! They cannot weary us with it; for it
seems as new as the sun, as remote as old Provence;
village, hill-side, vineyard, and chestnut wood shine in
the splendour of the word, the air is light, and white
things passing blind the eyes—a woman's linen, white
cattle, shining on the way from shadow to shadow. A
word of the sense of sight, and a summer word, in
short, compared with which the paraphrase is but a
picture. For *ensoleillé* I would claim the consent of all
readers—that they shall all acknowledge the spirit of
that French. But perhaps it is a mere personal pre-
ference that makes *le jour s'annonce* also sacred.

If the hymn "Stabat Mater dolorosa" was written
in Latin, this could be only that it might in time find
its true language and incomparable phrase at last—that
it might await the day of life in its proper German. I
found it there (and knew at once the authentic verse,
and knew at once for what tongue it had been really
destined) in the pages of the prayer-book of an apple-
woman at an Innsbruck church, and in the accents
of her voice.

A POINT OF BIOGRAPHY

THERE are few writers now—of the third class extremely few—who have not something sharp and sad to say about the cruelty of Nature; few who are able to attempt May in the woods without a modern reference to the manifold death and destruction with which the air, the branches, the mosses are said to be filled.

But no one has paused in the course of these phrases to take notice of the curious and conspicuous fact of the suppression of death and of the dead throughout this landscape of manifest life. Where are they—all the dying, all the dead, of the populous woods? Where do they hide their little last hours, where are they buried? Where is the violence concealed? Under what gay custom and decent habit? You may see, it is true, an earth-worm in a robin's beak, and may hear a thrush breaking a snail's shell; but these little things are, as it were, passed by with a kind of twinkle for apology, as by a well-bred man who does openly some little solecism which is too slight for direct mention, and which a meaner man might hide or avoid. Unless you are very modern indeed, you twinkle back at the bird.

But otherwise there is nothing visible of the havoc and the prey and plunder. It is certain that much of the visible life passes violently into other forms, flashes without pause into another flame; but not all. Amid all the killing there must be much dying. There are, for instance, few birds of prey left in our more accessible counties now, and many thousands of birds must die uncaught by a hawk and unpierced. But if their killing is done so modestly, so then is their dying also. Short lives have all these wild things, but there are innumerable flocks of them always alive; they must die, then, in innumerable flocks. And yet they keep the millions of the dead out of sight.

Now and then, indeed, they may be betrayed. It happened in a cold winter long ago. The late frosts were so sudden, and the famine was so complete, that the birds were taken unawares. The sky and the earth conspired, that February, to make known all the secrets; everything was published. Death was manifest. Editors, when a great man dies, are not more resolute than was the frost of '95.

The birds were obliged to die in public. They were surprised and forced to do thus. They became like Shelley in the monument which the art and imagination of England combined to raise to his memory at Oxford.

Frost was surely at work in both cases, and in both it wrought wrong. There is a similarity of unreason in betraying the death of a bird and in exhibiting the death of Shelley. The death of a soldier—*passe encore*. But the death of Shelley was not his goal. And the death of the birds is so little characteristic of them that, as has just been said, no one in the world is aware of their dying, except only in the case of birds in cages, who, again, are compelled to die with observation. The woodland is guarded and kept by a rule. There is no display of the battlefield in the fields. There is no tale of the game-bag, no boast. The hunting goes on, but with strange decorum. You may pass a fine season under the trees, and see nothing dead except here and there where a boy has been by, or a man with a trap, or a man with a gun. There is nothing like a butcher's shop in the woods.

But the biographers have always had other ways than those of the wild world. They will not have a man to die out of sight. I have turned over scores of "Lives," not to read them, but to see whether now and again there might be a "Life" which was not more emphatically a death. But there never is a modern biography that has taken the hint of Nature. One and all, these books have the disproportionate illness, the death out of all scale.

Even more wanton than the disclosure of a death is that of a mortal illness. If the man had recovered, his illness would have been rightly his own secret. But because he did not recover, it is assumed to be news for the first comer. Which of us would suffer the details of any physical suffering, over and done in our own lives, to be displayed and described? This is not a confidence we have a mind to make; and no one is authorized to ask for attention or pity on our behalf. The story of pain ought not to be told of us, seeing that by us it would assuredly not be told.

There is only one other thing that concerns a man still more exclusively, and that is his own mental illness, or the dreams and illusions of a long delirium. When he is in common language not himself, amends should be made for so bitter a paradox; he should be

allowed such solitude as is possibie to the alienated
spirit; he should be left to the "not himself," and
spared the intrusion against which he can so ill guard
that he could hardly have even resented it.

The double helplessness of delusion and death should
keep the door of an alienated poet's house, for example,
and refuse him to the reader. His mortal illness had
nothing to do with his poetry. Some rather affected objection is taken every now and then to the publication of
some facts(others being already well known) in the life of
Shelley. Nevertheless, these are all, properly speaking,
biography. What is not biography is the detail of the
accident of the manner of his death, the detail of his
cremation. Or if it was to be told—told briefly—it
was certainly not for marble. Shelley's death had no
significance, except inasmuch as he died young. It was
a detachable and disconnected incident. Ah, that was
a frost of fancy and of the heart that used it so, dealing
with an insignificant fact, and conferring a futile immortality. Those are ill-named biographers who seem
to think that a betrayal of the ways of death is a part
of their ordinary duty, and that if material enough for
a last chapter does not lie to their hand they are to
search it out. They, of all survivors, are called upon,
in honour and reason, to look upon a death with more
composure. To those who loved the dead closely, this
is, for a time, impossible; to them death becomes, for
a year, disproportionate; their dreams are fixed upon
it night by night. They have, in those dreams, to find
the dead in some labyrinth; they have to mourn his
dying and to welcome his recovery in such a mingling
of distress and of always incredulous happiness as is not

known even to dreams save in that first year of separation. But they are not biographers.

If death is the privacy of the woods, it is the more conspicuously secret because it is their only privacy. You may watch or may surprise everything else. The nest is retired, not hidden. The chase goes on everywhere. It is wonderful how the perpetual chase seems to cause no perpetual fear. The songs are all audible. Life is undefended, careless, alert, and noisy.

It is a happy thing that minor artists have ceased, or almost ceased, to paint dead birds. Time was when they did it continually in that English School of water-colour art, stippled, of which surrounding nations, it was agreed, were envious. They must have killed their bird to paint him, for he is not to be caught dead. A bird is more easily caught alive than dead.

A poet, on the contrary, is easily—too easily—caught dead. Minor artists now seldom stipple the bird on its back, but a good sculptor and a University together modelled their Shelley on his back, unessentially drowned; and everybody may read about the sick mind of a great poet.

THE HONOURS OF MORTALITY

THE brilliant talent which has quite lately and quite suddenly arisen, to devote itself to the use of the day or of the week, in illustrated papers—the enormous production of art in black and white—is assuredly a confession that the Honours of Mortality are worth working for. Fifty years ago, men worked for the honours of immortality; these were the commonplace of their ambition; they declined to attend to the beauty of things of use that were destined to be broken and worn out, and they looked forward to surviving themselves by painting bad pictures; so that what to do with their bad pictures in addition to our own has become the problem of the nation and of the householder alike. To-day men have begun to learn that their sons will be grateful to them for few bequests. Art consents at last to work upon the tissue and the china that are doomed to the natural and necessary end—destruction; and art shows a most dignified alacrity to do her best, daily, for the " process," and for oblivion.

Doubtless this abandonment of hopes so large at once and so cheap costs the artist something; nay, it implies an acceptance of the inevitable that is not less than heroic. And the reward has been in the singular and manifest increase of vitality in this work which is done for so short a life. Fittingly indeed does life reward the

48

acceptance of death, inasmuch as to die is to have been alive. There is a real circulation of blood—quick use, brief beauty, abolition, recreation. The honour of the day is for ever the honour of that day. It goes into the treasury of things that are honestly and completely ended and done with. And when can so happy a thing be said of a lifeless oil-painting? Who of the wise would hesitate? To be honourable for one day—one named and dated day, separate from all other days of the ages— or to be for an unlimited time tedious?

COMPOSURE

TRIBULATION, Immortality, the Multitude: what remedy of composure do these words bring for their own great disquiet! Without the remoteness of the Latinity the thought would come too close and shake too cruelly. In order to the sane endurance of the intimate trouble of the soul an aloofness of language is needful. Johnson feared death. Did his noble English control and postpone the terror? Did it keep the fear at some courteous, deferent distance from the centre of that human heart, in the very act of the leap and lapse of mortality? Doubtless there is in language such an educative power. Speech is a school. Every language is a persuasion, an induced habit, an instrument which receives the note indeed but gives the tone. Every language imposes a quality, teaches a temper, proposes a way, bestows a tradition: this is the tone—the voice —of the instrument. Every language, by counterchange, returns to the writer's touch or breath his own intention, articulate: this is his note. Much has always been said, many things to the purpose have been thought, of the power and the responsibility of the note. Of the legislation and influence of the tone I have been led to think by comparing the tranquillity of Johnson and the composure of Canning with the stimulated and close emotion, the interior trouble, of those

writers who have entered as disciples in the school of
the more Teutonic English.

For if every language be a school, more significantly
and more educatively is a part of a language a school to
him who chooses that part. Few languages offer the
choice. The fact that a choice is made implies the
results and fruits of a decision. The French author is
without these. They are of all the heritages of the
English writer the most important. He receives a
language of dual derivation. He may submit himself to
either University, whither he will take his impulse and
his character, where he will leave their influence, and
whence he will accept their re-education. The Frenchman has certainly a style to develop within definite
limits; but he does not subject himself to suggestions
tending mainly hitherwards or thitherwards, to currents
of various race within one literature. Such a choice of
subjection is the singular opportunity of the Englishman. I do not mean to ignore the necessary mingling.
Happily that mingling has been done once for all for us
all. Nay, one of the most charming things that a
master of English can achieve is the repayment of the
united teaching by linking their results so exquisitely
in his own practice, that words of the two schools are
made to meet each other with a surprise and delight
that shall prove them at once gayer strangers, and
sweeter companions, than the world knew they were.
Nevertheless there remains the liberty of choice as to
which school of words shall have the place of honour
in the great and sensitive moments of an author's
style: which school shall be used for conspicuousness,
and which for multitudinous service. And the choice

being open, the perturbation of the pulses and impulses of so many hearts quickened in thought and feeling in this day suggests to me a deliberate return to the recollectedness of the more tranquil language. "Doubtless there is a place of peace."

A place of peace, not of indifference. It is impossible not to charge some of the moralists of the eighteenth century with an indifference into which they educated their platitudes and into which their platitudes educated them. Addison thus gave and took, until he was almost incapable of coming within arm's-length of a real or spiritual emotion. There is no knowing to what distance the removal of the "appropriate sentiment" from the central soul might have attained but for the change and renewal in language, which came when it was needed. Addison had assuredly removed eternity far from the apprehension of the soul when his Cato hailed the "pleasing hope," the "fond desire"; and the touch of war was distant from him who conceived his "repulsed battalions" and his "doubtful battle." What came afterwards, when simplicity and nearness were restored once more, was doubtless journeyman's work at times. Men were too eager to go into the workshop of language. There were unreasonable raptures over the mere making of common words. "A hand-shoe! a finger-hat! a foreword! Beautiful!" they cried; and for the love of German the youngest daughter of Chrysale herself might have consented to be kissed by a grammarian. It seemed to be forgotten that a language with all its construction visible is a language little fitted for the more advanced mental processes; that its images are material; and that, on the other hand, a certain spiritualizing and subtilizing effect of alien derivations is a privilege and an advantage incalculable—that to possess that half of the language within which Latin heredities lurk and Romanesque allusions are at play is to possess the state and security of a dead tongue, without the death.

But now I spoke of words encountering as gay strangers, various in origin, divided in race, within a master's phrase. The most beautiful and the most sudden of such meetings are of course in Shakespeare. "Superfluous kings," "A lass unparalleled," "Multitudinous seas": we needed not to wait for the eighteenth century or for the nineteenth or for the twentieth to learn the splendour of such encounters, of such differences, of such nuptial unlikeness and union. But it is well that we should learn them afresh. And it is well, too, that we should not resist the rhythmic reaction bearing us now somewhat to the side of the Latin. Such a reaction is in some sort an ethical need for our day. We want to quell the exaggerated decision of monosyllables. We want the poise and the pause that imply vitality at times better than headstrong movement expresses it. And not the phrase only but the form of verse might render us timely service. The controlling couplet might stay with a touch a modern grief, as it ranged in order the sorrows of Canning for his son. But it should not be attempted without a distinct intention of submission on the part of the writer. The couplet transgressed against, trespassed upon, used loosely, is like a law outstripped, defied—to the dignity neither of the rebel nor of the rule.

To Letters do we look now for the guidance and

direction which the very closeness of the emotion taking us by the heart makes necessary. Shall not the
Thing more and more, as we compose ourselves to
literature, assume the honour, the hesitation, the leisure,
the reconciliation of the Word?

THE LITTLE LANGUAGE

DIALECT is the elf rather than the genius of place, and a dwarfish master of the magic of local things.

In England we hardly know what a concentrated homeliness it nourishes; inasmuch as, with us, the castes and classes for whom Goldoni and Gallina and Fogazzaro have written in the patois of the Veneto, use no dialect at all.

Neither Goldoni nor Gallina has charged the Venetian language with so much literature as to take from the people the shelter of their almost unwritten tongue. Signor Fogazzaro, bringing tragedy into the homes of dialect, does but show us how the language staggers under such a stress, how it breaks down, and resigns that office. One of the finest of the characters in the ranks of his admirable fiction is that old manageress of the narrow things of the house whose daughter is dying insane. I have called the dialect a shelter. This it is; but the poor lady does not cower within; her resigned head erect, she is shut out from that homely refuge, suffering and inarticulate. The two dramatists in their several centuries also recognized the inability of the dialect. They laid none but light loads upon it. They caused it to carry no more in their homely plays than it carries in homely life. Their work leaves it what it was—the talk of a people talking much about few things; a people like our own and any other in their lack of literature, but local and all Italian in their lack of silence.

Common speech is surely a greater part of life to such a people than to one less pleased with chatter or more pleased with books. I am writing of men, women, and children (and children are not forgotten, since we share a patois with children on terms of more than common equality) who possess, for all occasions of ceremony and opportunities of dignity, a general, national, liberal, able, and illustrious tongue, charged with all its history and all its achievements; for the speakers of dialect, of a certain rank, speak Italian, too. But to tamper with their dialect, or to take it from them, would be to leave them houseless and exposed in their daily business. So much does their patois seem to be their refuge from the heavy and multitudinous experiences of a literary tongue, that the stopping of a fox's earth might be taken as the image of any act that should spoil or stop the talk of the associated seclusion of their town, and leave them in the bleakness of a larger patriotism.

The Venetian people, the Genoese, and the other speakers of languages that might all have proved right "Italian" had not Dante, Petrarch, and Boccaccio written in Tuscan, can neither write nor be taught hard things in their dialect, although they can live, whether easy lives or hard, and evidently can die, therein. The hands and feet that have served the villager and the citizen at homely tasks have all the lowliness of his patois, to his mind; and when he must perforce yield up their employment, we may believe that it is a simple thing to die in so simple and so narrow a language, one so comfortable, neighbourly, tolerant, and compassionate; so confidential; so incapable, ignorant, unappalling, inapt to wing any wearied thought upon difficult flight or to spur it upon hard travelling.

Not without words is mental pain, or even physical pain, to be undergone; but the words that have done no more than order the things of the narrow street are not words to put a fine edge or a piercing point to any human pang. It may even well be that to die in dialect is easier than to die in the eloquence of Manfred, though that declaimed language, too, is doubtless a defence, if one of a different manner.

These writers in Venetian—they are named because in no other Italian dialect has work so popular as Goldoni's been done, nor so excellent as Signor Fogazzaro's—have left the unlettered local language in which they loved to deal, to its proper limitations. They have not given weighty things into its charge, nor made it heavily responsible. They have added nothing to it; nay, by writing it they might even be said to have made it duller, had it not been for the reader and the actor. Insomuch as the intense expressiveness of a dialect—of a small vocabulary in the mouth of a dramatic people—lies in the various accent wherewith a southern citizen knows how to enrich his talk, it remains for the actor to restore its life to the written phrase. In dialect the author is forbidden to search for the word, for there is none lurking for his choice; but of tones, of allusions, and of references and inferences of the voice, the speaker of dialect is a master. No range of phrases can be his, but he has the more or the less confidential inflection, until at times the close communication of the narrow street becomes a very conspiracy.

Let it be borne in mind that dialect properly so called is something all unlike, for instance, the mere jargon of London streets. The difference may be measured by the fact that Italian dialects have a highly organized and orderly grammar. The Londoner cannot keep the small and loose order of the grammar of good English; the Genoese conjugates his patois verbs, with subjunctives and all things of that handsome kind, lacked by the English of Universities.

The middle class—the *piccolo mondo*—that shares Italian dialect with the poor are more strictly local in their manners than either the opulent or the indigent of the same city. They have moreover the busy intelligence (which is the intellect of patois) at its keenest. Their speech keeps them a sequestered place which is Italian, Italian beyond the ken of the traveller, and beyond the reach of alteration. And—what is pretty to observe—the speakers are well conscious of the characters of this intimate language. An Italian countryman who has known no other climate will vaunt, in fervent platitudes, his Italian sun; in like manner he is conscious of the local character of his language, and tucks himself within it at home, whatever Tuscan he may speak abroad. A properly spelt letter, Swift said, would seem to expose him and Mrs. Dingley and Stella to the eyes of the world; but their little language, ill-written, was "snug."

Lovers have made a little language in all times; finding the greater language insufficient, do they ensconce themselves in the smaller? discard noble and literary speech as not noble enough, and in despair thus prattle and gibber and stammer? Rather perhaps this departure from English is but an excursion after gaiety. The ideal lovers, no doubt, would be so simple as to be grave; that is a tenable opinion. Nevertheless, age by age they have been gay; and age by age they have exchanged language imitated from the children they doubtless never studied, and perhaps never loved. Why so? They might have chosen broken English of other sorts—that, for example, which was once thought amusing in farce, as spoken by the Frenchman conceived by the Englishman—a complication of humour fictitious enough, one might think, to please anyone; or else a fragment of negro dialect; or the style of telegrams; or the masterly adaptation of the simple savage's English devised by Mrs. Plornish in her intercourse with the Italian. But none of these found favour. The choice has always been of the language of children. Let us suppose that the flock of winged Loves worshipping Venus in the Titian picture, and the noble child that rides his lion erect with a background of Venetian gloomy dusk, may be the inspirers of those prattlings. " See then thy selfe likewise art lyttle made," says Spenser's Venus to her child.

Swift was the best prattler. He had caught the language, surprised it in Stella when she was veritably a child. He did not push her clumsily back into a childhood he had not known; he simply prolonged in her a childhood he had loved. He is "seepy." "Nite, dealest dea, nite dealest logue." It is a real good-night. It breathes tenderness from that moody and uneasy bed of projects.

A COUNTERCHANGE

IL s'est trompé de défunte. The writer of this phrase had his sense of that portly manner of French, and his burlesque is fine; but—the paradox must be risked —because he was French he was not able to possess all its grotesque mediocrity to the full; that is reserved for the English reader. The words are in the mouth of a widower who, approaching his wife's tomb, perceives there another *monsieur*. *Monsieur*, again; the French reader is deprived of the value of this word, too, in its place; it says little or nothing to him, whereas the Englishman, who has no word of the precise *bourgeois* significance that it sometimes bears, but who must use one of two English words of different allusion—man or gentleman—knows the exact value of its commonplace. The serious Parisian, then, sees *un autre monsieur*; as it proves anon, there had been a divorce in the history of the lady, but the later widower is not yet aware of this, and explains to himself the presence of *un monsieur* in his own place by that weighty phrase, *Il s'est trompé de défunte.*

The strange effect of a thing so charged with allusion and with national character is to cause an English reader to pity the mocking author who was debarred by his own language from possessing the whole of his own comedy. It is, in fact, by contrast with his English that an Englishman does possess it. Your

official, your professional Parisian has a vocabulary of
enormous, unrivalled mediocrity. When the novelist
perceives this he does not perceive it all, because some
of the words are the only words in use. Take an
author at his serious moments, when he is not at all
occupied with the comedy of phrases, and he now and
then touches a word that has its burlesque by mere
contrast with English. "L'Histoire d'un Crime," of
Victor Hugo, has so many of these touches as to be,
by a kind of reflex action, a very school of English.
The whole incident of the omnibus in that grave work
has unconscious international comedy. The Deputies
imprisoned in the interior of the omnibus had been, it
will be remembered, shut out of their Chamber by the
perpetrator of the *Coup d'Etat*, but each had his official
scarf. Scarf—pish!—*l'écharpe! Ceindre l'écharpe*—there
is no real English equivalent. Civic responsibility never
was otherwise adequately expressed. An indignant
deputy passed his scarf through the window of the
omnibus, as an appeal to the public, *et l'agita*. It is a
pity that the French reader, having no simpler word, is
not in a position to understand the slight burlesque.
Nay, the mere word "public," spoken with this peculiar
French good faith, has for us I know not what untransferable gravity.

There is, in short, a general international counterchange. It is altogether in accordance with our actual
state of civilization, with its extremely "specialized"
manner of industry, that one people should make a
phrase, and another should have and enjoy it. And, in
fact, there are certain French authors to whom should
be secured the use of the literary German whereof

Germans, and German women in particular, ought with all severity to be deprived. For Germans often tell you of words in their own tongue that are untranslatable; and accordingly they should not be translated, but given over in their own conditions, unaltered, into safer hands. There would be a clearing of the outlines of German ideas, a better order in the phrase; the possessors of an alien word, with the thought it secures, would find also their advantage.

So with French humour. It is expressly and signally for English ears. It is so even in the commonest farce. The unfortunate householder, for example, who is persuaded to keep walking in the conservatory *pour rétablir la circulation*, and the other who describes himself *sous-chef de bureau dans l'enregistrement*, and he who proposes to *faire hommage* of a doubtful turbot to the neighbouring *employé de l'octroi*—these and all their like speak commonplaces so usual as to lose in their own country the perfection of their dullness. We only, who have the alternative of plainer and fresher words, understand it. It is not the least of the advantages of our own dual English that we become sensible of the mockery of certain phrases that in France have lost half their ridicule, uncontrasted.

Take again the common rhetoric that has fixed itself in conversation in all Latin languages—rhetoric that has ceased to have allusions, either majestic or comic. To the ear somewhat unused to French this proffers a frequent comedy that the well-accustomed ear, even of an Englishman, no longer detects. A guard on a French railway, who advised two travellers to take a certain train for fear they should be obliged to *végéter* for a whole hour in the waiting-room of such or such a station seemed to the less practised tourist to be a fresh kind of unexpected humourist.

One of the phrases always used in the business of charities and subscriptions in France has more than the intentional comedy of the farce-writer; one of the most absurd of his personages, wearying his visitors in the country with a perpetual game of bowls, says to them: *Nous jouons cinquante centimes—les bénéfices seront versés intégralement à la souscription qui est ouverte à la commune pour la construction de notre maison d'école.*

Flétrir, again Nothing could be more rhetorical than this perfectly common word of controversy. The comic dramatist is well aware of the spent violence of this phrase, with which every serious Frenchman will reply to opponents, especially in public matters. But not even the comic dramatist is aware of the last state of refuse commonplace that a word of this kind represents. Refuse rhetoric, by the way, rather than Emerson's "fossil poetry," would seem to be the right name for human language as some of the processes of the several recent centuries have left it.

The French comedy, then, is fairly stuffed with things for an Englishman. They are not all, it is true, so finely comic as *Il s'est trompé de défunte.* In the report of that dull, incomparable sentence there is enough humour, and subtle enough, for both the maker and the reader; for the author who perceives the comedy as well as custom will permit, and for the reader who takes it with the freshness of a stranger. But if not so keen as this, the current word of French comedy is of the same quality of language. When of the fourteen

couples to be married by the mayor, for instance, the
deaf clerk has shuffled two, a looker-on pronounces:
Il s'est empétré dans les futurs. But for a reader who
has a full sense of the several languages that exist in
English at the service of the several ways of human
life, there is, from the mere terminology of official
France, high or low—daily France—a gratuitous and
uncovenanted smile to be had. With this the wit of
the report of French literature has little to do. Nor is
it in itself, perhaps, reasonably comic, but the slightest
irony of circumstance makes it so. A very little of
the mockery of conditions brings out all the latent
absurdity of the *sixième et septième arrondissements,* in the
twinkling of an eye. So is it with the mere *domicile*;
with the aid of but a little of the burlesque of life, the
suit at law to *réintégrer le domicile conjugal* becomes as
grotesque as a phrase can make it. Even *à domicile*
merely—the word of every shopman—is, in the unconscious mouths of the speakers, always awaiting the
lightest touch of farce, if only an Englishman hears it;
so is the advice of the police that you shall *circuler* in
the street; so is the request, posted up, that you shall
not, in the churches.

So are the serious and ordinary phrases, *maison
nuptiale, maison mortuaire,* and the still more serious
repos dominical, oraison dominicale. There is no majesty
in such words. The unsuspicious gravity with which
they are spoken broadcast is not to be wondered at,
the language offering no relief of contrast; and what
is much to the credit of the comic sensibility of literature is the fact that, through this general unconsciousness, the sensibility of a thousand authors of comedy

perceives the fun, and singles out the familiar thing, and compels that most elaborate dullness to amuse us. *Us*, above all, by virtue of the custom of counterchange here set forth.

Who shall say whether, by operation of the same exchange, the English poets that so persist in France may not reveal something within the English language —one would be somewhat loth to think so—reserved to the French reader peculiarly? Byron to the multitude, Edgar Poe to the select? Then would some of the mysteries of French reading of English be explained otherwise than by the plainer explanation that has hitherto satisfied our haughty curiosity. The taste for rhetoric seemed to account for Byron, and the desire of the rhetorician to claim a taste for poetry seemed to account for Poe. But, after all, *patatras*! Who can say?

HARLEQUIN MERCUTIO

THE first time that Mercutio fell upon the English stage, there fell with him a gay and hardly human figure; it fell, perhaps finally, for English drama. That manner of man—Arlecchino, or Harlequin—had out-lived his playmates, Pantaleone, Brighella, Colombina, and the Clown. A little of Pantaleone survives in old Capulet, a little in the father of the Shrew, but the life of Mercutio in the one play, and of the subordinate Tranio in the other—both Harlequins—is less quickly spent, less easily put out, than the smouldering of the old man. Arlecchino frolics in and out of the tragedy and comedy of Shakespeare, until he thus dies in his lightest, his brightest, his most vital shape, Mercutio.

Arlecchino, the tricksy and shifty spirit, the contriver, the busybody, the trusty rogue, the wonder-worker, the man in disguise, the mercurial one, lives on buoy-antly in France to the age of Molière. He is officious and efficacious in the skin of Mascarille and Ergaste and Scapin; but he tends to be a lacquey, with a refer-ence rather to Antiquity and the Latin comedy than to the Middle Ages, as on the English stage his mere memory survives differently to a later age in the person of "Charles, his friend." What convinces me that he virtally died with Mercutio is chiefly this—that this comrade of Romeo's lives so keenly as to be fully capable of the death that he takes at Tybalt's sword-

point; he lived indeed, he dies indeed. Another thing
that marks a close of a career of ages is his loss of his
long customary good luck. Who ever heard of Arlecchino unfortunate before, at fault with his sword-play,
overtaken by tragedy? His time had surely come. The
gay companion was to bleed; Tybalt's sword had made
a way. 'Twas not so deep as a well nor so wide as a
church-door, but it served.

Some confusion comes to pass among the typical
figures of the primitive Italian play, because Harlequin,
on that conventional little stage of the past, has a hero's
place, whereas when he interferes in human affairs he
is only the auxiliary. He might be lover and bridegroom
on the primitive stage, in the comedy of these few and
unaltered types; but when Pantaloon, Clown, and
Harlequin play with really human beings, then Harlequin can be no more than a friend of the hero, the
friend of the bridegroom. The five figures of the old
stage dance attendance; they play around the business
of those who have the dignity of mortality; they, poor
immortals—a clown who does not die, a pantaloon never
far from death, who yet does not die, a Columbine who
never attains Desdemona's death of innocence, or
Juliet's death of rectitude and passion—flit in the
backward places of the stage.

Ariel fulfils his office, and is not of one kind with
those he serves. Is there a memory of Harlequin in
that delicate figure? Something of the subservient immortality, of the light indignity, proper to Pantaleone,
Brighella, Arlecchino, Colombina, and the Clown,
hovers away from the stage when Ariel is released from
the trouble of human things.

Immortality, did I say? It was immortality until
Mercutio fell. And if some claim be made to it still
because Harlequin has transformed so many scénes for
the pleasure of so many thousand children, since Mercutio died, I must reply that our modern Harlequin is
no more than a *marionnette*; he has returned whence
he came. A man may play him, but he is—as he was
first of all—a doll. From doll-hood Arlecchino took
life, and, so promoted, flitted through a thousand com-
edies, only to be again what he first was; save that, as
once a doll played the man, so now a man plays the
doll. It is but a memory of Arlecchino that our children see, a poor statue or image endowed with mobility
rather than with life.

With Mercutio vanished the light heart that had
given to the serious ages of the world an hour's refuge
from the unforgotten burden of responsible conscience; the light heart assumed, borrowed,
made dramatically the spectator's own.
We are not serious now, and no
heart now is quite light, even
for an hour.'

COMMENTARIES

LAUGHTER

TIMES have been, it is said, merrier than these; but it is certain nevertheless that laughter never was so honoured as now; were it not for the paradox one might say, it never was so grave. Everywhere the joke "emerges"—as an "elegant" writer might have it—emerges to catch the attention of the sense of humour; and everywhere the sense of humour wanders, watches, and waits to honour the appeal.

It loiters, vaguely but perpetually willing. It wears (let the violent personification be pardoned) a hanging lip, and a wrinkle in abeyance, and an eye in suspense. It is much at the service of the vagrant encounterer, and may be accosted by any chance daughters of the game. It stands in untoward places, or places that were once inappropriate, and is early at some indefinite appointment, some ubiquitous tryst, with the compliant jest.

All literature becomes a field of easy assignations; there is a constant signalling, an endless recognition. Forms of approach are remitted. And the joke and the sense of humour, with no surprise of meeting, or no gaiety of strangeness, so customary has the promiscuity become, go up and down the pages of the paper and the book. See, again, the theatre. A somewhat easy sort of comic acting is by so much the best thing upon

73

our present stage that little else can claim—paradox again apart—to be taken seriously.

There is, in a word, a determination, an increasing tendency, away from the Oriental estimate of laughter as a thing fitter for women, fittest for children, and unfitted for the beard. Laughter is everywhere and at every moment proclaimed to be the honourable occupation of men, and in some degree distinctive of men, and no mean part of their prerogative and privilege. The sense of humour is chiefly theirs, and those who are not men are to be admitted to the jest upon their explanation. They will not refuse explanation. And there is little upon which a man will so value himself as upon that sense, " in England, now."

Assuredly it would be a pity if laughter should ever become, like rhetoric and the arts, a habit. And it is in some sort a habit when it is not inevitable. If we ask ourselves why we laugh, we must confess that we laugh oftenest because—being amused—we intend to show that we are amused. We are right to make the sign, but a smile would be as sure a signal as a laugh, and more sincere; it would but be changing the convention; and the change would restore laughter itself to its own place. We have fallen into the way of using it to prove something—our sense of the goodness of the jest, to wit; but laughter should not thus be used, it should go free. It is not a demonstration, whether in logic, or—as the word demonstration is now generally used—in emotion; and we do ill to charge it with that office.

Something of the Oriental idea of dignity might not be amiss among such a people as ourselves containing

wide and numerous classes who laugh without cause:
audiences; crowds; a great many clergymen, who perhaps first fell into the habit in the intention of proving
that they were not gloomy; but a vast number of lay-
men also who had not that excuse; and many women
who laugh in their uncertainty as to what is humorous
and what is not. This last is the most harmless of all
kinds of superfluous laughter. When it carries an
apology, a confession of natural and genial ignorance,
and when a gentle creature laughs a laugh of hazard
and experiment, she is to be more than forgiven. What
she must not do is to laugh a laugh of instruction, and
as it were retrieve the jest that was never worth the
taking.

There are, also, a few women who do not disturb
themselves as to a sense of humour, but who laugh
from a sense of happiness. Childish is that trick, and
sweet. For children, who always laugh because they
must, and never by way of proof or sign, laugh only
half their laughs out of their sense of humour; they
laugh the rest under a mere stimulation: because of
abounding breath and blood; because some one runs
behind them, for example, and movement does so jog
their spirits that their legs fail them, for laughter, without a jest.

If ever the day should come when men and women
shall be content to signal their perception of humour
by the natural smile, and shall keep the laugh for its
own unpremeditated act, shall laugh seldom, and simply,
and not thrice at the same thing—once for foolish surprise, and twice for tardy intelligence, and thrice to let
it be known that they are amused—then it may be

time to persuade this laughing nation not to laugh so loud as it is wont in public. The theatre audiences of louder-speaking nations laugh lower than ours. The laugh that is chiefly a signal of the laugher's sense of the ridiculous is necessarily loud; and it has the disadvantage of covering what we may perhaps wish to hear from the actors. It is a public laugh, and no ordinary citizen is called upon for a public laugh. He may laugh in public, but let it be with private laughter there.

Let us, if anything like a general reform be possible in these times of dispersion and of scattering, keep henceforth our sense of humour in a place better guarded, as something worth a measure of seclusion. It should not loiter in wait for the alms of a joke in adventurous places. For the sense of humour has other things to do than to make itself conspicuous in the act of laughter. It has negative tasks of valid virtue; for example, the standing and waiting within call of tragedy itself, where, excluded, it may keep guard.

No reasonable man will aver that the Oriental manners are best. This would be to deny Shakespeare as his comrades knew him, where the wit " out-did the meat, out-did the frolic wine," and to deny Ben Jonson's " tart Aristophanes, neat Terence, witty Plautus," and the rest. Doubtless Greece determined the custom for all our Occident; but none the less might the modern world grow more sensible of the value of composure.

To none other of the several powers of our souls do we so give rein as to this of humour, and none other do we indulge with so little fastidiousness. It is as though there were honour in governing the other senses, and honour in refusing to govern this. It is as though we were ashamed of reason here, and shy of dignity, and suspicious of temperance, and diffident of moderation, and too eager to thrust forward that which loses nothing by seclusion.

THE RHYTHM OF LIFE

IF life is not always poetical, it is at least metrical.
Periodicity rules over the mental experience of man,
according to the path of the orbit of his thoughts. Distances are not gauged, ellipses not measured, velocities
not ascertained, times not known. Nevertheless, the
recurrence is sure. What the mind suffered last week,
or last year, it does not suffer now; but it will suffer
again next week or next year. Happiness is not a matter of events; it depends upon the tides of the mind.
Disease is metrical, closing in at shorter and shorter
periods towards death, sweeping abroad at longer and
longer intervals towards recovery. Sorrow for one
cause was intolerable yesterday, and will be intolerable
to-morrow; to-day it is easy to bear, but the cause has
not passed. Even the burden of a spiritual distress un-
solved is bound to leave the heart to a temporary
peace; and remorse itself does not remain—it returns.
Gaiety takes us by a dear surprise. If we had made a
course of notes of its visits, we might have been on the
watch, and would have had an expectation instead of a
discovery. No one makes such observations; in all the
diaries of students of the interior world, there have
never come to light the records of the Kepler of such
cycles. But Thomas à Kempis knew of the recurrences, if he did not measure them. In his cell alone
with the elements—" What wouldst thou more than

these? for out of these were all things made "—he learnt the stay to be found in the depth of the hour of bitterness, and the remembrance that restrains the soul at the coming of the moment of delight, giving it a more conscious welcome, but presaging for it an inexorable flight. And "rarely, rarely comest thou," sighed Shelley, not to Delight merely, but to the Spirit of Delight. Delight can be compelled beforehand, called, and constrained to our service—Ariel can be bound to a daily task; but such artificial violence throws life out of metre, and it is not the spirit that is thus compelled. *That* flits upon an orbit elliptically or parabolically or hyperbolically curved, keeping no man knows what trysts with Time.

It seems fit that Shelley and the author of the "Imitation" should both have been keen and simple enough to perceive these flights, and to guess at the order of this periodicity. Both souls were in close touch with the spirits of their several worlds, and no deliberate human rules, no infractions of the liberty and law of the universal movement, kept from them the knowledge of recurrences. *Eppur si muove.* They knew that presence does not exist without absence; they knew that what is just upon its flight of farewell is already on its long path of return. They knew that what is approaching to the very touch is hastening towards departure. "O wind," cried Shelley, in autumn,

> O wind,
> If winter comes can spring be far behind?

They knew that the flux is equal to the reflux; that to interrupt with unlawful recurrences, out of time, is to

weaken the impulse of onset and retreat; the sweep
and impetus of movement. To live in constant efforts
after an equal life, whether the equality be sought in
mental production, or in spiritual sweetness, or in the
joy of the senses, is to live without either rest or full
activity. The souls of certain of the saints, being singularly simple and single, have been in the most complete
subjection to the law of periodicity. Ecstasy and de-
solation visited them by seasons. They endured, during
spaces of vacant time, the interior loss of all for which
they had sacrificed the world. They rejoiced in the
uncovenanted beatitude of sweetness alighting in their
hearts. Like them are the poets whom, three times or
ten times in the course of a long life, the Muse has
approached, touched, and forsaken. And yet hardly
like them; not always so docile, nor so wholly prepared for the departure, the brevity, of the golden and
irrevocable hour. Few poets have fully recognized the
metrical absence of their Muse. For full recognition is
expressed in one only way—silence.

It has been found that several tribes in Africa and in
America worship the moon, and not the sun; a great
number worship both; but no tribes are known to adore
the sun, and not the moon. On her depend the tides;
and she is Selene, mother of Herse, bringer of the dews
that recurrently irrigate lands where rain is rare. More
than any other companion of earth is she the Measurer.
Early Indo-Germanic languages knew her by that name.
Her metrical phases are the symbol of the order of recurrence. Constancy in approach and in departure is
the reason of her inconstancies. Juliet will not receive a
vow spoken in invocation of the moon; but Juliet did

not live to know that love itself has tidal times—lapses
and ebbs which are due to the metrical rule of the interior heart, but which the lover vainly and unkindly
attributes to some outward alteration in the beloved.
For man—except those elect already named—is hardly
aware of periodicity. The individual man either never
learns it fully, or learns it late. And he learns it so
late, because it is a matter of cumulative experience upon
which cumulative evidence is long lacking. It is in the
after-part of each life that the law is learnt so definitely
as to do away with the hope or fear of continuance.
That young sorrow comes so near to despair is a result
of this young ignorance. So is the early hope of great
achievement. Life seems so long, and its capacity so
great, to one who knows nothing of all the intervals it
needs must hold—intervals between aspirations, between actions, pauses as inevitable as the pauses of sleep.
And life looks impossible to the young unfortunate, un-
aware of the inevitable and unfailing refreshment. It
would be for their peace to learn that there is a tide in
the affairs of men, in a sense more subtle—if it is not
too audacious to add a meaning to Shakespeare—than
the phrase was meant to contain. Their joy is flying
away from them on its way home; their life will wax
and wane; and if they would be wise, they must wake
and rest in its phases, knowing that they are ruled by
the law that commands all things—a sun's revolutions
and the rhythmic pangs of maternity.

DOMUS ANGUSTA

THE narrow house is a small human nature compelled to a large human destiny, charged with a
fate too great, a history too various, for its slight cap-
acities. Men have commonly complained of fate; but
their complaints have been of the smallness, not of the
greatness, of the human lot. A disproportion—all in
favour of man—between man and his destiny is one of
the things to be taken for granted in literature: so
frequent and so easy is the utterance of the habitual
lamentation as to the trouble of a " vain capacity," so
well explained has it ever been.

> Thou hast not half the power to do me harm
> That I have to be hurt,

discontented man seems to cry to Heaven, taking the
words of the brave Emilia. But inarticulate has been
the voice within the narrow house. Obviously it never
had its poet. Little elocution is there, little argument
or definition, little explicitness. And yet for every vain
capacity we may assuredly count a thousand vain des-
tinies, for every liberal nature a thousand liberal fates.
It is the trouble of the wide house we hear of, clamorous of its disappointments and desires. The narrow
house has no echoes; yet its pathetic shortcoming

82

might well move pity. On that strait stage is acted a
generous tragedy; to that inadequate soul is intrusted
an enormous sorrow; a tempest of movement makes
its home within that slender nature; and heroic happiness seeks that timorous heart.

We may, indeed, in part know the narrow house by
its inarticulateness—not, certainly, its fewness of words,
but its inadequacy and imprecision of speech. For,
doubtless, right language enlarges the soul as no other
power or influence may do. Who, for instance, but
trusts more nobly for knowing the full word of his
confidence? Who but loves more penetratingly for possessing the ultimate syllable of his tenderness? There
is a " pledging of the word," in another sense than the
ordinary sense of troth and promise. The poet pledges
his word, his sentence, his verse, and finds therein a
peculiar sanction. And I suppose that even physical
pain takes on an edge when it not only enforces a pang
but whispers a phrase. Consciousness and the word are
almost as closely united as thought and the word.
Almost—not quite; in spite of its inexpressive speech,
the narrow house is aware and sensitive beyond, as it
were, its poor power.

But as to the whole disparity between the destiny
and the nature, we know it to be general. Life is great
that is trivially transmitted; love is great that is vul-
garly experienced. Death, too, is a heroic virtue; and
to the keeping of us all is death committed: death,
submissive in the indocile, modest in the fatuous,
several in the vulgar, secret in the familiar. It is destructive, because it not only closes but contradicts
life. Unlikely people die. The one certain thing, it is

also the one improbable. A dreadful paradox is perhaps wrought upon a little nature that is incapable of death and yet is constrained to die. That is a true destruction, and the thought of it is obscure.

Happy literature corrects all this disproportion by its immortal pause. It does not bid us follow man or woman to an illogical conclusion. Mrs. Micawber never does desert Mr. Micawber. Considering her mental powers, by the way, an illogical conclusion for her would be manifestly inappropriate. Shakespeare, indeed, having seen a life whole, sees it to an end: sees it out, and Falstaff dies. More than Promethean was the audacity that, having kindled, quenched that spark. But otherwise the grotesque man in literature is immortal, and with something more significant than the immortality awarded to him in the sayings of rhetoric; he is perdurable because he is not completed. His humours are strangely matched with perpetuity. But, indeed, he is not worthy to die; for there is something graver than to be immortal, and that is to be mortal. I protest I do not laugh at man or woman in the world. I thank my fellow mortals for their wit, and also for the kind of joke that the French so pleasantly call *une joyeuseté*; these are to smile at. But the gay injustice of laughter is between me and the man or woman in a book, in fiction, or on the stage in a play.

That narrow house—there is sometimes a message from its living windows. Its bewilderment, its reluctance, its defect, show by moments from eyes that are apt to express none but common things. There are allusions unawares, involuntary appeals, in those brief glances. Far from me and from my friends be the misfortune of meeting such looks in reply to pain of our inflicting. To be clever and sensitive and to hurt the foolish and the stolid—"wouldst thou do such a deed for all the world?"

INNOCENCE AND EXPERIENCE

I SHALL not ask the commentators whether Blake used these two words in union or in antithesis. They assuredly have an inseverable union in the art of literature. The songs of Innocence and Experience are for each poet the songs of his own separate heart and life; but to take the cumulative experiences of other men, and to use these in place of the virginal fruit of thought—whereas one would hardly consent to take them for ordering even the most habitual of daily affairs —is to forgo Innocence and Experience at once and together. Obviously, Experience can be nothing except personal and separate; and Innocence of a singularly solitary quality is his who does not dip his hands into other men's histories, and does not give to his own word the common sanction of other men's summaries and conclusions. Therefore I bind Innocence and Experience in one, and take them as a sign of the necessary and noble isolation of man from man—of his uniqueness. But if I had a mind to forgo that manner of personal separateness, and to use the things of others, I think I would rather appropriate their future than their past. Let me put on their hopes, and the colours of their confidence, if I must borrow. Not that I would burden my prophetic soul with unjustified ambitions; but even this would be more tolerable than to load my memory with an unjustifiable history.

86

And yet how differently do the writers of a certain kind of love-poetry consider this matter. These are the love-poets who have no reluctance in adopting the past of a multitude of people to whom they have not even been introduced. Their verse is full of ready-made memories, various, numerous, and cruel. No single life —supposing it to be a liberal life concerned with something besides sex—could quite suffice for so much experience, so much disillusion, so much *déception*. To achieve that tone in its fullness it is necessary to take for one's own the *praeterita* (say) of Alfred de Musset and of the men who helped him—not to live but—to have lived; it is necessary to have lived much more than any man lives, and to make a common hoard of erotic remembrances with all kinds of poets.

As the Franciscans wear each other's old habits, and one friar goes about darned because of another's rending, so the poet of a certain order grows cynical for the sake of many poets' old loves. Not otherwise will the resultant verse succeed in implying so much—or rather so many, in the feminine plural. The man of very sensitive individuality might hesitate at the adoption. The Franciscan is understood to have a fastidiousness and to overcome it. And yet, if choice were, one might wish rather to make use of one's fellow men's old shoes than put their old secrets to use, and dress one's art in a motley of past passions. Moreover, to utilize the mental experience of many is inevitably to use their verse and phrase. For the rest, all the traits of this love-poetry are familiar enough. One of them is the absence of the word of promise and pledge, the loss of the earliest and simplest of the impulses of love: which is the vow. "Till death!" "For ever!" are cries too simple and too natural to be commonplace, and in their denial there is the least tolerable of banalities—that of other men's disillusions.

Perfect personal distinctness of Experience would be in literature a delicate Innocence. Not a passage of cheapness, of greed, of assumption, of sloth, or of any such sins in the work of him whose love-poetry were thus true, and whose *pudeur* of personality thus simple and inviolate. This is the private man, in other words the gentleman, who will neither love nor remember in common.

THE HOURS OF SLEEP

THERE are hours claimed by Sleep, but refused to him. None the less are they his by some state within the mind, which answers rhythmically and punctually to that claim. Awake and at work, without drowsiness, without languor, and without gloom, the night mind of man is yet not his day mind; he has night-powers of feeling which are at their highest in dreams, but are night's as well as sleep's. The powers of the mind in dream, which are inexplicable, are not altogether baffled because the mind is awake; it is the hour of their return as it is the hour of a tide's, and they do return.

In sleep they have their free way. Night then has nothing to hamper her influence, and she draws the emotion, the senses, and the nerves of the sleeper. She urges him upon those extremities of anger and love, contempt and terror, to which not only can no event of the real day persuade him, but for which, awake, he has perhaps not even the capacity. This increase of capacity, which is the dream's, is punctual to the night, even though sleep and the dream be kept at arm's length.

The child, not asleep, but passing through the hours of sleep and their dominions, knows that the mood of night will have its hour; he postpones his troubled heart, and will answer it another time, in the other state, by

89

day. "I shall be able to bear this when I am grown up" is not oftener in a young child's mind than "I shall endure to think of it in the day-time." By this he confesses the double habit and double experience, not to be interchanged, and communicating together only by memory and hope.

Perhaps it will be found that to work all by day or all by night is to miss something of the powers of a complex mind. One might imagine the rhythmic experience of a poet, subject, like a child, to the time, and tempering the extremities of either state by messages of remembrance and expectancy.

Never to have had a brilliant dream, and never to have had any delirium, would be to live too much in the day; and hardly less would be the loss of him who had not exercised his waking thought under the influence of the hours claimed by dreams. And as to choosing between day and night, or guessing whether the state of day or dark is the truer and the more natural, he would be rash who should make too sure.

In order to live the life of night, a watcher must not wake too much. That is, he should not alter so greatly the character of night as to lose the solitude, the visible darkness, or the quietude. The hours of sleep are too much altered when they are filled by lights and crowds; and Nature is cheated so, and evaded, and her rhythm broken, as when the larks caged in populous streets make ineffectual springs and sing daybreak songs when the London lamps are lighted. Nature is easily deceived; and the muse, like the lark, may be set all astray as to the hour. You may spend the peculiar hours of sleep amid so much noise and among

so many people that you shall not be aware of them;
you may thus merely force and prolong the day. But
to do so is not to live well both lives; it is not to yield
to the daily and nightly rise and fall, cradled in the
swing of change.

There surely never was a poet but was now and
then rocked in such a cradle of alternate hours. "It
cannot be," says Herbert, "that I am he on whom
Thy tempests fell all night."

It is in the hours of sleep that the mind, by some
divine paradox, has the extremest sense of light.
Almost the most shining lines in English poetry—lines
that cast sunrise shadows—are those of Blake, written
confessedly from the side of night, the side of sorrow
and dreams, and those dreams the dreams of little
chimney-sweepers; all is as dark as he can make it
with the "bags of soot"; but the boy's dream of the
green plain and the river is too bright for day. So, indeed, is another brightness of Blake's, which is also, in
his poem, a child's dream, and was certainly conceived
by him in the hours of sleep, in which he woke to
write the Songs of Innocence:

> O what land is the land of dreams?
> What are its mountains, and what are its streams?
> O father, I saw my mother there,
> Among the lilies by waters fair.
> Among the lambs clothèd in white,
> She walk'd with her Thomas in sweet delight.

To none but the hours claimed and inspired by sleep,
held awake by sufferance of sleep, belongs such a
vision.

Corot also took the brilliant opportunity of the

hours of sleep. In some landscapes of his early manner
he has the very light of dreams, and it was surely because he went abroad at the time when sleep and
dreams claimed his eyes that he was able to see so
spiritual an illumination. Summer is precious for a
painter, chiefly because in summer so many of the
hours of sleep are also hours of light. He carries the
mood of man's night out into the sunshine—Corot did
so—and lives the life of night, in all its genius, in the
presence of a risen sun. In the only time when the
heart can dream of light, in the night of visions, with
the rhythmic power of night at its dark noon in his
mind, his eyes see the soaring of the actual sun.

He himself has not yet passed at that hour into the
life of day. To that life belongs many another kind of
work, and a sense of other kinds of beauty; but the
summer daybreak was seen by Corot with the extreme
perception of the life of night. Here, at last, is the
explanation of all the memories of dreams recalled by
these visionary paintings, done in earlier years than
were those, better known, that are the Corots of all
the world. Every man who knows what it is to dream
of landscape meets with one of these works of Corot's
first manner with a cry, not of welcome only, but of recognition. Here is morning perceived by the spirit of
the hours of sleep.

SOLITUDE

THE wild man is alone at will, and so is the man for whom civilization has been kind. But there are the multitudes to whom civilization has given little but its reaction, its rebound, its chips, its refuse, its shavings, sawdust, and waste, its failures; to them solitude is a right forgone or a luxury unattained; a right forgone, we may name it, in the case of the nearly savage, and a luxury unattained in the case of the nearly refined. These has the movement of the world thronged together into some blind by-way.

Their share in the enormous solitude which is the common, unbounded, and virtually illimitable possession of all mankind has lapsed, unclaimed. They do not know it is theirs. Of many of their kingdoms they are ignorant, but of this most ignorant. They have not guessed that they own for every man a space inviolate, a place of unhidden liberty and of no obscure enfranchisement. They do not claim even the solitude of closed corners, the narrow privacy of the lock and key; nor could they command so much. For the solitude that has a sky and a horizon they know not how to wish.

It lies in a perpetual distance. England has leagues thereof, landscapes, verge beyond verge, a thousand thousand places in the woods, and on uplifted hills. Or rather, solitudes are not to be measured by miles;

they are to be numbered by days. They are freshly and freely the dominion of every man for the day of his possession. There is loneliness for innumerable solitaries. As many days as there are in all the ages, so many solitudes are there for men. This is the open house of the earth; no one is refused. Nor is the space shortened or the silence marred because, one by one, men in multitudes have been alone there before. Solitude is separate experience. Nay, solitudes are not to be numbered by days, but by men themselves. Every man of the living and every man of the dead might have had his " privacy of light."

It needs no park; it is to be found in the merest working country; and a thicket may be as secret as a forest. It is not so difficult to get for a time out of sight and earshot. Even if your solitude be enclosed, it is still an open solitude, so there be " no cloister for the eyes," and a space of far country or a cloud in the sky be privy to your hiding-place. But the best solitude does not hide at all.

This the people who have drifted together into the streets live whole lives and never know. Do they suffer from their deprivation of even the solitude of the hiding-place? There are many who never have a whole hour alone. They live in reluctant or indifferent companionship, as people may in a boarding-house, familiar with one another and not intimate. They live under careless observation and subject to a vagabond curiosity. Theirs is the involuntary and perhaps the unconscious loss which is futile and barren.

One knows the men, and the many women, who have sacrificed all their solitude to the perpetual society of the school, the cloister, or the hospital ward. They walk without secrecy, candid, simple, visible, without moods, unchangeable, in a constant communication and practice of action and speech. Theirs assuredly is no barren or futile loss, and they have a conviction, and they bestow the conviction, of solitude deferred.

Who has painted solitude so that the solitary seemed to stand alone and inaccessible? There is the loneliness of the shepherdess in many a drawing of J. F. Millet. The little figure is away, aloof. The girl stands so when the painter is gone. She waits so on the sun for the closing of the hours of pasture. Millet has her as she looks, out of sight.

Now, although solitude is a prepared, secured, defended, elaborate possession of the rich, they too deny themselves the natural solitude of a woman with a child. A newly-born child is so nursed and talked about, handled and jolted and carried about by aliens, and there is so much importunate service going forward, that a woman is hardly alone long enough to become aware how her own blood in her child moves separately, beside her, with another rhythm and different pulses. All is commonplace until the doors are closed upon the two. This unique intimacy at night is a profound retreat, an absolute seclusion. It is more than single solitude; it is a redoubled isolation more remote than mountains, safer than valleys, deeper than forests, and further than mid-sea.

That solitude partaken—the only partaken solitude in the world—is the Point of Honour of ethics. Treachery to that obligation and a betrayal of that confidence might well be held to be the least pardonable of all crimes. There is no innocent sleep so innocent as sleep shared between a woman and a child, the little breath hurrying beside the longer, as a child's foot runs. But the favourite crimé of the sentimentalist is that of a woman against her child. Her power, her intimacy, her opportunity, that should be her accusers, are held to excuse her. She gains the most slovenly of indulgences, on the vulgar plea that her crime was easy. Compassion is due to her on another ground, but not excuse on this.

Lawless and vain art of a certain kind is apt to claim to-day, by the way, some such fondling as a heroine of the dock receives from common opinion. The vain artist had all the advantages. He was master of his own purpose, such as it was; it was his secret, and the public was not privy to his conscience. He does violence to the obligations of which he is aware, and which the world does not know very explicitly. Nothing is easier. Or he is lawless in a more literal sense, but only hopes the world will believe that he has a whole code of his own making. It would, nevertheless, be less unworthy to break obvious rules obviously in the obvious face of the public, and to abide the common rebuke.

It has just been said that a park is by no means necessary for the preparation of a country solitude. Indeed, to make those far and wide and long approaches and avenues to peace seems to be a denial of the accessibility of what should be so simple. A step, a pace or so aside, is enough to lead thither.

A park insists too much, and, besides, does not insist very sincerely. In order to fulfil the apparent professions and to keep the published promise of a park, the owner thereof should be a lover of long seclusion or of a very life of loneliness. He should have gained the state of solitariness which is a condition of life quite unlike any other. The traveller who may have gone astray in countries where an almost lifelong solitude is possible knows how invincibly apart are the lonely figures he has seen in desert places there. Their loneliness is broken by his passage, it is true, but hardly so to them. They look at him, but they are not aware that he looks at them. Nay, they look at him as though they were invisible. Their un-self-consciousness is absolute; it is in the wild degree. They are solitaries, body and soul; even when they are curious, and turn to watch the passer-by, they are essentially alone. Now, no one ever found that attitude in a squire's figure, or that look in any country gentleman's eyes. The squire is not a lifelong solitary; he never bore himself as though he were invisible. He never had the impersonal ways of a herdsman in the remoter Apennines, with a blind, blank hut in the rocks for his dwelling. Millet would not even have taken him as a model for a solitary in the briefer and milder sylvan solitudes of France. And yet nothing but a lifelong, habitual, and wild solitariness would be quite proportionate to a park of any magnitude.

If there is a look of human eyes that tells of perpetual loneliness, so there is also the familiar look that is the sign of perpetual crowds. It is the London expression, and, in its way, the Paris expression. It is the quickly caught, though not interested, look, the dull but ready glance of those who do not know of their forfeited place apart; who have neither the open secret nor the close; no reserve, no need of refuge, no flight nor impulse of flight; no moods but what they may brave out in the street, no hope of news from solitary counsels.

DECIVILIZED

THE difficulty of dealing—in the course of any critical duty—with decivilized man lies in this: when you accuse him of vulgarity—sparing him no doubt the word—he defends himself against the charge of barbarism. Especially from new soil — remote, colonial—he faces you, bronzed, with a half conviction of savagery, partly persuaded of his own youthfulness of race. He writes, and recites, poems about ranches and canyons; they are designed to betray the recklessness of his nature and to reveal the good that lurks in the lawless ways of a young society. He is there to explain himself, voluble, with a glossary for his own artless slang. But his colonialism is only provincialism very articulate. The new air does but make old decadences seem more stale; the young soil does but set into fresh conditions the ready-made, the uncostly, the refuse feeling of a race decivilizing. He who played long this pattering part of youth, hastened to assure you with so self-denying a face he did not wear war-paint and feathers, that it became doubly difficult to communicate to him that you had suspected him of nothing wilder than a second-hand (figurative) dress coat. And when it was a question not of rebuke, but of praise, even the American was ill-content with the word of the judicious who lauded him for some delicate successes in continuing something of the literature of England,

something of the art of France; he was more eager for
the applause that stimulated him to write poems in prose
form and to paint panoramic landscape, after brief train-
ing in academies of native inspiration. Even now
English voices are constantly calling upon America to
begin—to begin, for the world is expectant. Whereas
there is no beginning for her, but instead a fine and
admirable continuity which only a constant care can
guide into sustained advance.

But decivilized man is not peculiar to new soil. The
English town, too, knows him in all his dailiness. In
England, too, he has a literature, an art, a music, all his
own—derived from many and various things of price.
Trash, in the fullness of its insimplicity and cheapness,
is impossible without a beautiful past. Its chief characteristic—which is futility, not failure—could not be
achieved but by the long abuse, the rotatory repro-
duction, the quotidian disgrace, of the utterances of
Art, especially the utterance by words. Gaiety, vigour,
vitality, the organic quality, purity, simplicity, precision
—all these are among the antecedents of trash. It is
after them; it is also, alas, because of them. And
nothing can be much sadder that such a proof of what
may possibly be the failure of derivation.

Evidently we cannot choose our posterity. Reversing
the steps of time, we may, indeed choose backwards.
We may give our thoughts noble forefathers. Well
begotten, well born our fancies must be; they shall be
also well derived. We have a voice in decreeing our
inheritance, and not our inheritance only, but our
heredity. Our minds may trace upwards and follow
their ways to the best well-heads of the arts. The very

habit of our thoughts may be persuaded one way unawares by their antenatal history. Their companions
must be lovely, but need be no lovelier than their
ancestors; and being so fathered and so husbanded,
our thoughts may be intrusted to keep the counsels of
literature.

Such is our confidence in a descent we know. But,
of a sequel which of us is sure? Which of us is secured
against the dangers of subsequent depreciation? And,
moreover, which of us shall trace the contemporary
tendencies, the one towards honour, the other towards
dishonour? Or who shall discover why derivation becomes degeneration, and where and when and how the
bastardy befalls? The decivilized have every grace as
the antecedent of their vulgarities, every distinction as
the precedent of their mediocrities. No ballad-concert
song, feign it sigh, frolic, or laugh, but has the excuse
that the feint was suggested, was made easy, by some
living sweetness once. Nor are the decivilized to blame
as having in their own persons possessed civilization
and marred it. They did not possess it; they were born
into some tendency to derogation, into an inclination
for things mentally inexpensive. And the tendency
can hardly do other than continue.

Nothing can look duller than the future of this
second-hand and multiplying world. Men need not be
common merely because they are many; but the in-
fection of commonness once begun in the many, what
dullness in their future! To the eye that has reluctantly
discovered this truth—that the vulgarized are not *un*-
civilized, and that there is no growth for them—it does
not look like a future at all. More ballad-concerts, more

quaint English, more robustious barytone songs, more piecemeal pictures, more colonial poetry, more young nations with withered traditions. Yet it is before this prospect that the provincial overseas lifts up his voice in a boast or a promise common enough among the incapable young, but pardonable only in senility. He promises the world a literature, an art, that shall be new because his forest is untracked and his town just built. But what the newness is to be he cannot tell. Certain words were dreadful once in the mouth of desperate old age. Dreadful and pitiable as the threat of an impotent king, what shall we name them when they are the promise of an impotent people? "I will do such things: what they are yet I know not."

WAYFARING

THE SPIRIT OF PLACE

WITH mimicry, with praises, with echoes, or with answers, the poets have all but outsung the bells. The inarticulate bell has found too much interpretation, too many rhymes professing to close with her inaccessible utterance, and to agree with her remote tongue. The bell, like the bird, is a musician pestered with literature.

To the bell, moreover, men do actual violence. You cannot shake together a nightingale's notes, or strike or drive them into haste, nor can you make a lark toll for you with intervals to suit your turn, whereas wedding-bells are compelled to seem gay by mere movement and hustling. I have known some grim bells, with not a single joyous note in the whole peal, so forced to hurry for a human festival, with their harshness made light of, as though the Bishop of Hereford had again been forced to dance in his boots by a merry highway-man.

The clock is an inexorable but less arbitrary player than the bellringer, and the chimes await their appointed time to fly—wild prisoners—by twos or threes, or in greater companies. Fugitives—one or twelve taking wing—they are sudden, they are brief, they are gone; they are delivered from the close hands of this actual present. Not in vain is the sudden upper door opened against the sky; they are away, hours of the past.

Of all unfamiliar bells, those which seem to hold the memory most surely after but one hearing are bells of an unseen cathedral of France when one has arrived by night; they are no more to be forgotten than the bells in " Parsifal." They mingle with the sound of feet in unknown streets, they are the voices of an unknown tower; they are loud in their own language. The spirit of place, which is to be seen in the shapes of the fields and the manner of the crops, to be felt in a prevalent wind, breathed in the breath of the earth, overheard in a far street-cry or in the tinkle of some blacksmith, calls out and peals in the cathedral bells. It speaks its local tongue remotely, steadfastly, largely, clamorously, loudly, and greatly by these voices; you hear the sound in its dignity, and you know how familiar, how childlike, how lifelong it is in the ears of the people. The bells are strange, and you know how homely they must be. Their utterances are, as it were, the classics of a dialect.

Spirit of place! It is for this we travel, to surprise its subtlety; and where it is a strong and dominant angel, that place, seen once, abides entire in the memory with all its own accidents, its habits, its breath, its name. It is recalled all a lifetime, having been perceived a week, and is not scattered but abides, one living body of remembrance. The untravelled spirit of place—not to be pursued, for it never flies, but always to be disdiscovered, never absent, without variation—lurks in the by-ways and rules over the towers, indestructible, an indescribable unity. It awaits us always in its ancient and eager freshness. It is sweet and vivacious within its immemorial boundaries, but it never crosses them. Long white roads outside have mere suggestions of it and prophecies; they give promise not of its coming, for it abides, but of a new and singular and unforeseen goal for our present pilgrimage, and of an intimacy to be made. Was ever journey too hard or too long that had to pay such a visit? And if by good fortune it is a child who is the pilgrim, the spirit of place gives him a peculiar welcome, for antiquity and the conceiver of antiquity (who is only a child) know one another; nor is there a more delicate perceiver of locality than a child. He is well used to words and voices that he does not understand, and this is a condition of his simplicity; and when those unknown words are bells, loud in the night, they are to him as homely and as old as lullabies.

If, especially in England, we make rough and reluctant bells go in gay measures, when we whip them to run down the scale to ring in a wedding—bells that would step to quite another and a less agile march with a better grace—there are belfries that hold far sweeter companies. If there is no music within Italian churches, there is a most curious local immemorial music in many a campanile on the heights. Their way is for the ringers to play a tune on the festivals, and the tunes are not hymn tunes or popular melodies, but proper bell-tunes, made for bells. Doubtless they were made in times better versed than ours in the subdivisions of the arts, and better able to understand the strength that lies ready in the mere little submission to the means of a little art, and to the limits—nay, the very embarrassments—of those means. If it were but possible to give here a real bell-tune—which cannot be, for those melodies are rather long—the reader would understand how some village musician of the past used his narrow means as a composer for the bells, with what freshness, completeness, significance, fancy, and what effect of liberty.

These hamlet-bells are the sweetest, as to their own voices, in the world. When I speak of their antiquity I use the word relatively. The belfries are no older than the fifteenth or sixteenth century, the time when Italy seems to have been generally rebuilt. But, needless to say, this is antiquity for music, especially in Italy. At that time they must have had foundries for bells of tender voices, and pure, warm, light, and golden throats, precisely tuned. The hounds of Theseus had not a more just scale, tuned in a peal, than a North Italian belfry holds in leash. But it does not send them out in a mere scale, it touches them in the order of the game of a charming melody. Of all cheerful sounds made by man this is by far the most light-hearted. You do not hear it from the great churches. Giotto's coloured tower in Florence, that carries the bells for Santa Maria del Fiore and Brunelleschi's dome, does not ring more than four contralto notes, tuned with sweetness, depth, and dignity, and swinging one musical phrase which softly fills the country.

The village belfry it is that grows so fantastic and has such delicate bells. Obviously it stands alone with its own village, and can therefore hear its own tune from beginning to end. There are no other bells in earshot. Other such dovecote-doors are suddenly set open to the cloud, on a *festa* morning, to let fly those soft-voiced flocks, but the nearest is behind one of many mountains, and our local tune is uninterrupted. Doubtless this is why the little, secluded, sequestered art of composing melodies for bells—charming division of an art, having its own ends and means, and keeping its own wings for unfolding by law—dwells in these solitary places. No tunes in a town would get this hearing, or would be made clear to the end of their frolic amid such a wide and lofty silence.

Nor does every inner village of Italy hold a bell-tune of its own; the custom is Ligurian. Nowhere so much as in Genoa does the nervous tourist complain of church bells in the morning, and in fact he is made to hear an honest rout of them betimes. But the nervous tourist has not, perhaps, the sense of place, and the genius of place does not signal to him to go and find it among innumerable hills, where one by one, one by one, the belfries stand and play their tunes. Variable are those lonely melodies, having a differing gaiety for the festivals; and a pitiful air is played for the burial of a villager.

As for the poets, there is but one among so many of their bells that seems to toll with a spiritual music so loud as to be unforgotten when the mind goes up a little higher than the earth, to listen in thought to earth's untethered sounds. This is Milton's curfew, that sways across one of the greatest of all the seashores of poetry—" the wide-watered."

POPULAR BURLESQUE

THE more I consider that strange inversion of idolatry which is the motive of Guy Fawkes Day and which annually animates the by-streets with the sound of processionals and of recessionals—a certain popular version of "Lest we forget" their unvaried theme; the more I hear the cries of derision raised by the makers of this likeness of something unworshipful on the earth beneath, so much the more am I convinced that the national humour is that of banter, and that no other kind of mirth so gains as does this upon the public taste.

Here, for example, is the popular idea of a street festival; that day is as the people will actually have it, with their own invention, their own material, their own means, and their own spirit. They owe nothing on this occasion to the promptings or the subscriptions of the classes that are apt to take upon themselves the direction and tutelage of the people in relation to any form of art. Here on every fifth of November the people have their own way with their own art; and their way is to offer the service of the image-maker, reversed in hissing and irony, to some creature of their hands.

It is a wanton fancy; and perhaps no really barbarous people is capable of so overturning the innocent plan of original portraiture. To make a mental

image of all things that are named to the ear, or conceived in the mind, being an industrious custom of
children and childish people which lapses in the age of
much idle reading, the making of a material image is
the still more diligent and more sedulous act, whereby
primitive man controls and caresses his own fancy.
The savage may take arms anon, disappointed, against
his own work; but did he ever do that work in malice
from the outset?

From the statue to the doll, images are all outraged
in the person of the guy. If it were but an antithesis
to the citizen's idea of something admirable which he
might carry in procession on some other day, the
carrying of the guy would be less gloomy; but he would
hoot at a suspicion that he might admire anything so
much as to make a good-looking doll in its praise.
There is absolutely no image-making art in the practice of our people, except only this art of rags and
contumely. Or, again, if the revenge taken upon a
guy were that of anger for a right cause, the destruction would not be the work of so thin an annual
malice and of so heartless a rancour.

But the single motive is that popular irony which
becomes daily—or so it seems—more and more the
holiday temper of the majority. Mockery is the only
animating impulse, and a loud incredulity is the only
intelligence. They make an image of someone in
whom they do not believe, to deride it. Say that the
guy is the effigy of an agitator in the cause of something to be desired; the street man and boy have then
two motives of mocking: they think the reform to be
not worth doing, and they are willing to suspect the

reformer of some kind of hypocrisy. Perhaps the guy of this occasion is the most characteristic of all guys in London. The people, having him or her to deride, do not even wait for the opportunity of their annual procession. They anticipate time, and make an image when it is not November, and sell it at the market of the kerb.

Hear, moreover, the songs which some nameless one makes for the citizens, perhaps in thoughtful renunciation of the making of their laws. These, too, seem to have for their inspiration the universal taunt. They are, indeed, most in vogue when they have no meaning at all—this it is that makes the *succès fou* (and here Paris is of one mind with London) of the street ; but short of such a triumph, and when a meaning is discernible, it is an irony.

Bank Holiday courtship (if the inappropriate word can be pardoned) seems to be done, in real life, entirely by banter. And it is the strangest thing to find that the banter of women by men is the most mocking in the exchange. If the irony of the maid's tongue is provocative, that of the man's is derisive. Somewhat of the order of things as they stood before they were inverted seems to remain, nevertheless, as a memory; nay, to give the inversion a kind of lagging interest. Irony is made more complete by the remembrance, and by an implicit allusion to the state of courtship in other classes, countries, or times. Such an allusion no doubt gives all its peculiar twang to the burlesque of love.

With the most strange submission these English-women in their millions undergo all degrees of derision from the tongues of men who are their mates, equals, contemporaries, perhaps in some obscure sense, their suitors, and in a strolling manner, with one knows not what ungainly motive of reserve, even their admirers. Nor from their tongues only; for, to pass the time, the holiday swain annoys the girl; and if he wears her hat, it is ten to one that he has plucked it off with a humorous disregard of her dreadful pins.

We have to believe that unmocked love has existence in the streets, because of the proof that is published when a man shoots a woman who has rejected him; and from this also do we learn to believe that a woman of the burlesque classes is able to reject. But for that sign we should find little or nothing intelligible in what we see or overhear of the drama of love in popular life.

In its easy moments, in its leisure, at holiday time, it baffles all tradition, and shows us the spirit of comedy clowning after a fashion that is insular and not merely civic. You hear the same twang in country places; and whether the English maid, having, like the antique, thrown her apple at her shepherd, run into the thickets of Hampstead Heath or among sylvan trees, it seems that the most humorous thing to be done by the swain would be, in the opinion in vogue, to stroll another way. Insular I have said, because I have not seen the like of this fashion whether in America or elsewhere in Europe. But the chief inversion of all, proved summarily by the annual inversion of the worship of images on the fifth of November, is that of a sentence of Wordsworth's—"We live by admiration."

HAVE PATIENCE, LITTLE SAINT

SOME considerable time must have gone by since any kind of courtesy ceased, in England, to be held necessary in the course of communication with a beggar. Feeling may be humane, and the interior act most gentle; there may be a tacit apology, and a profound misgiving unexpressed; a reluctance not only to refuse but to be arbiter; a dislike of the office; a regret, whether for the unequal distribution of social luck or for a purse left at home, equally sincere; howbeit custom exacts no word or sign, nothing whatever of intercourse. If a dog or a cat accosts you, or a calf in a field comes close to you with a candid infant face and breathing nostrils of investigation, or if any kind of animal comes to you on some obscure impulse of friendly approach, you acknowledge it. But the beggar to whom you give nothing expects no answer to a question, no recognition of his presence, not so much as the turn of your eyelid in his direction, and never a word to excuse you.

Nor does this blank behaviour seem savage to those who are used to nothing else. Yet it is somewhat more inhuman to refuse an answer to the beggar's remark than to leave a shop without "Good morning." When complaint is made of the modern social manner—that it has no merit but what is negative, and that it is apt even to abstain from courtesy with more lack of grace than the abstinence absolutely requires—the habit of manners towards beggars is probably not so much as thought of. To the simply human eye, however, the prevalent manner towards beggars is a striking thing; it is significant of so much.

Obviously it is not easy to reply to begging except by the intelligible act of giving. We have not the ingenuous simplicity that marks the caste answering more or less to that of Vere de Vere, in Italy, for example. An elderly Italian lady on her slow way from her own ancient ancestral *palazzo* to the village, and accustomed to meet, empty-handed, a certain number of beggars, answers them by a retort which would be, literally translated, " Excuse me, dear; I, too, am a poor devil," and the last word she naturally puts into the feminine.

Moreover, the sentence is spoken in all the familiarity of the local dialect—a dialect that puts any two people at once upon equal terms as nothing else can do it. Would it were possible to present the phrase to English readers in all its own helpless good-humour. The excellent woman who uses it is practising no eccentricity thereby, and raises no smile. It is only in another climate, and amid other manners, that one cannot recall it without a smile. To a mind having a lively sense of contrast it is not a little pleasant to imagine an elderly lady of corresponding station in England replying so to importunities for alms; albeit we have nothing answering to the good fellowship of a broad patois used currently by rich and poor, and yet slightly grotesque in the case of all speakers—a dialect in which, for example, no sermon is ever preached, and in which no book is ever printed, except for fun; a dialect "familiar, but by no means vulgar." Besides, even if our Englishwoman could by any possibility bring herself to say to a mendicant, "Excuse me, dear; I, too, am a poor devil," she would still not have the opportunity of putting the last word punctually into the feminine, which does so complete the character of the sentence.

The phrase at the head of this paper is the far more graceful phrase of excuse customary in the courteous manners of Portugal. And everywhere in the South, where an almost well-dressed old woman, who suddenly begins to beg from you when you least expected it, calls you "my daughter," you can hardly reply without kindness. Where the tourist is thoroughly well known, doubtless the company of beggars are used to savage manners in the rich; but about the byways and remoter places there must still be some dismay at the anger, the silence, the indignation, and the inexpensive haughtiness wherewith the opportunity of alms-giving is received by travellers.

In nothing do we show how far the West is from the East so emphatically as we show it by our lofty ways towards those who so manifestly put themselves at our feet. It is certainly not pleasant to see them there; but silence or a storm of impersonal protest—a protest that appeals vaguely less to the beggars than to some not impossible police—does not seem the most appropriate manner of rebuking them. We have, it may be, a scruple on the point of human dignity,

compromised bv the entreaty and the thanks of the
mendicant; but we have a strange way of vindicating
that dignity when we refuse to man, woman, or child
the recognition of a simply human word. Nay, our
offence is much the greater of the two. It is not
merely a rough and contemptuous intercourse, it is the
refusal of intercourse—the last outrage. How do we
propose to redress those conditions of life that annoy
us when a brother whines, if we deny the presence, the
voice, and the being of this brother, and if, because
fortune has refused him money, we refuse him existence?

We take the matter too seriously, or not seriously
enough, to hold it in the indifference of the wise.
"Have patience, little saint," is a phrase that might
teach us the cheerful way to endure our own unintelligible fortunes in the midst, say, of the population of a
hill-village among the most barren of the Maritime
Alps, where huts of stone stand among the stones of
an unclothed earth, and there is no sign of daily bread.
The people, albeit unused to travellers, yet know by
instinct what to do, and beg without the delay of a
moment as soon as they see your unwonted figure.
Let it be taken for granted that you give all you can;
some form of refusal becomes necessary at last, and the
gentlest—it is worth while to remember—is the most
effectual. An indignant tourist, one who to the portent
of a puggaree which, perhaps, he wears on a gray day,
adds that of ungovernable rage, is so wild a visitor that
no attempt at all is made to understand him; and the
beggars beg dismayed but unalarmed, uninterruptedly,
without a pause or a conjecture. They beg by rote,

thinking of something else, as occasion arises, and all indifferent to the violence of the rich.

It is the merry beggar who has so lamentably disappeared. If a beggar is still merry anywhere, he hides away what it would so cheer and comfort us to see; he practises not merely the conventional seeming, which is hardly intended to convince, but a more subtle and dramatic kind of semblance, of no good influence upon the morals of the road. He no longer trusts the world with a sight of his gaiety. He is not a whole-hearted mendicant, and no longer keeps that liberty of unstable balance whereby an unattached creature can go in a new direction with a new wind. The merry beggar was the only adventurer free to yield to the lighter touches of chance, the touches that a habit of resistance has made imperceptible to the seated and stable social world.

The visible flitting figure of the unfettered madman sprinkled our literature with mad songs, and even one or two poets of to-day have, by tradition, written them; but that wild source of inspiration has been stopped; it has been built over, lapped and locked, imprisoned, led underground. The light melancholy and the wind-blown joys of the song of the distraught, which the poets were once ingenious to capture, have ceased to sound one note of liberty in the world's ears. But it seems that the grosser and saner freedom of the happy beggar is still the subject of a Spanish song.

That song is gay, not defiant; it is not an outlaw's or a robber's, it is not a song of violence or fear. It is the random trolling note of a man who owes his liberty to no disorder, failure, or ill-fortune, but takes it by choice from the voluntary world, enjoys it at the hand of unreluctant charity; who twits the world with its own choice of bonds, but has not broken his own by force. It seems, therefore, the song of an indomitable liberty of movement, light enough for the puffs of a zephyr chance.

AT MONASTERY GATES

NO woman has ever crossed the inner threshold, or shall ever cross it, unless a queen, English or foreign, should claim her privilege. Therefore, if a woman records here the slighter things visible of the monastic life, it is only because she was not admitted to see more than beautiful courtesy and friendliness were able to show her in guest-house and garden.

The Monastery is of fresh-looking Gothic, by Pugin —the first of the dynasty: it is reached by the white roads of a limestone country, and backed by a young plantation, and it gathers its group of buildings in a cleft high up among the hills of Wales. The brown habit is this, and these are the sandals, that come and go by hills of finer, sharper, and loftier line, edging the dusk and dawn of an Umbrian sky. Just such a Via Crucis climbs the height above Orta, and from the foot of its final crucifix you can see the sunrise touch the top of Monte Rosa, while the encircled lake below is cool with the last of the night. The same order of friars keep that sub-Alpine Monte Sacro, and the same have set the Kreuzberg beyond Bonn with the same steep path by the same fourteen chapels, facing the Seven Mountains and the Rhine.

Here, in North Wales, remote as the country is, with the wheat green over the blunt hill-tops, and the sky vibrating with larks, a long wing of smoke lies round the horizon. The country, rather thinly and languidly cultivated above, has a valuable sub-soil, and is burrowed with mines; the breath of pit and factory, out of sight, thickens the lower sky, and lies heavily over the sands of Dee. It leaves the upper blue clear and the head of Orion, but dims the flicker of Sirius and shortens the steady ray of the evening star. The people scattered about are not mining people, but half-hearted agriculturists, and very poor. Their cottages are rather cabins; not a tiled roof is in the country, but the slates have taken some beauty with time, having dips and dimples, and grass upon their edges. The walls are all thickly whitewashed, which is a pleasure to see. How willingly would one swish the harmless whitewash over more than half the colour—over all the chocolate and all the blue—with which the buildings of the world are stained! You could not wish for a better, simpler, or fresher harmony than whitewash makes with the slight sunshine and the bright gray of an English sky.

The gray-stone, gray-roofed monastery looks young in one sense—it is modern; and the friars look young in another—they are like their brothers of an earlier time. No one, except the journalists of yesterday, would spend upon them those tedious words, "quaint," or "old world." No such weary adjectives are spoken here, unless it be by the excursionists.

With large aprons tied over their brown habits, the Lay Brothers work upon their land, planting parsnips in rows, or tending a prosperous bee-farm. A young Friar, who sang the High Mass yesterday, is gaily hang-

ing the washed linen in the sun. A printing press, and
a machine which slices turnips, are at work in an out-
house, and the yard thereby is guarded by a St. Bernard,
whose single evil deed was that under one of the obscure
impulses of a dog's heart—atoned for by long and self-
conscious remorse—he bit the poet; and tried, says one
of the friars, to make doggerel of him. The poet,[1] too,
lives at the monastery gates, and on monastery ground,
in a seclusion which the tidings of the sequence of his
editions hardly reaches. There is no disturbing renown
to be got among the cabins of the Flintshire hills.
Homeward, over the verge, from other valleys, his light
figure flits at nightfall, like a moth.

To the coming and going of the friars, too, the
village people have become well used, and the infrequent excursionists, for lack of intelligence and of any
knowledge that would refer to history, look at them
without obtrusive curiosity. It was only from a Salvation Army girl that you heard the brutal word of contempt. She had come to the place with some companions, and with them was trespassing, as she was
welcome to do, within the monastery grounds. She
stood, a figure for Bournemouth pier, in her grotesque
bonnet, and watched the son of the Umbrian saint—
the friar who walks among the Giotto frescoes at
Assisi and between the cypresses of Bello Sguardo, and
has paced the centuries continually since the coming
of the friars. One might have asked of her the kindness of a fellow-feeling. She and he alike were so
habited as to show the world that their life was aloof
from its " idle business." By some such phrase, at least,

[1] Francis Thompson.

the friar would assuredly have attempted to include her in any spiritual honours ascribed to him. Or one might have asked of her the condescension of forbearance. "Only fancy," said the Salvation Army girl, watching the friar out of sight, "only fancy making such a fool of oneself!"

The great hood of the frairs, which is drawn over the head in Zurbaran's ecstatic picture, is turned to use when the friars are busy. As a pocket it relieves the over-burdened hands. A bottle of the local white wine, made by the brotherhood at Genoa, and sent to this house by the West, is carried in the cowl as a present to the stranger at the gates. The friars tell how a brother resolved, at Shrovetide, to make pancakes, and not only to make, but also to toss them. Those who chanced to be in the room stood prudently aside, and the brother tossed boldly. But that was the last that was seen of his handiwork. Victor Hugo sings in "La Légende des Siècles" of disappearance as the thing which no creature is able to achieve: here the impossibility seemed to be accomplished by quite an ordinary and a simple pancake. It was clean gone, and there was an end of it. Nor could any explanation of this ceasing of a pancake from the midst of the visible world be so much as divined by the spectators. It was only when the brother, in church, knelt down to meditate and drew his cowl about his head that the accident was explained.

Every midnight the sweet contralto bells call the community, who get up gaily to this difficult service. Of all duties this one never grows easy or familiar, and therefore never habitual. It is something to have found but one act aloof from habit. It is not merely that the friars overcome the habit of sleep. The subtler point is that they can never acquire the habit of sacrificing sleep. What art, what literature, or what life but would gain a secret security by such a point of perpetual freshness and perpetual initiative? It is not possible to get up at midnight without a will that is new night by night. So should the writer's work be done, and, with an intention perpetually unique, the poet's.

The contralto bells have taught these Western hills the "Angelus" of the French fields, and the hour of night—*l' ora di notte*—which rings with so melancholy a note from the village belfries on the Adriatic littoral, when the latest light is passing. It is the prayer for the dead: "Out of the depths have I cried unto Thee, O Lord."

The little flocks of novices, on paschal evenings, are folded to the sound of that evening prayer. The care of them is the central work of the monastery, which is placed in so remote a country because it is principally a place of studies. So much elect intellect and strength of heart withdrawn from the traffic of the world! True, the friars are not doing the task which Carlyle set mankind as a refuge from despair. These "bearded counsellors of God" keep their cells, read, study, suffer, sing, hold silence; whereas they might be "operating"— beautiful word!—upon the Stock Exchange, or painting Academy pictures, or making speeches, or reluctantly jostling other men for places. They might be among the involuntary busybodies who are living by futile tasks the need whereof is a discouraged fiction. There is absolutely no limit to the superfluous activities, to the art, to the literature, implicitly renounced by the dwellers within such walls as these. The output—again a beautiful word—of the age is lessened by this abstention. None the less hopes the stranger and pilgrim to pause and knock once again upon those monastery gates.

THE SEA WALL

A SINGULAR love of walls is mine; perhaps because of long living in London, with its too many windows and too few walls, the city which of all capitals takes least visible hold upon the ground. Walls, blank and strong, reaching outward at the base, are a satisfaction to the eyes teased by the inexpressive peering of windows, by that weak lapse and shuffling which is the London "area," and by the weak hollows of shop-fronts.

A wall is the safeguard of simplicity. It lays a long level line among the indefinite chances of the landscape. But never more majestic than in face of the wild sea, the wall, steadying its slanting foot upon the rock, builds in the serried ilex-wood and builds out the wave. The sea-wall is the wall at its best. And fine as it is on the strong coast, it is beautiful on the weak littoral and the imperilled levels of a northern beach.

That sea wall is low and long; sea-pinks grow on the salt grass that passes away into shingle at its foot. It is at close quarters with the tempestuous sea, when, from the low coast with its low horizon, the sky-line of sea is jagged. Never from any height does the ocean-horizon show thus broken and battered at its very verge, but from the flat coast and the narrow world you can see the wave as far as you can see the water; and the stormy light of a clear horizon is seen to be

126

mobile and shifting with the buoyant hillocks and their restless line.

The Dutch dyke has not that English aspect of a lowly parapet against a tide; it springs with a look of haste and of height; and when you first run upstairs from the encumbered Dutch fields to look at the sea, you are apt, because of old rivalries, to make comparisons with England. Even the Englishman of to-day is apt to share something of the old national perversity that was minded to cast derision upon the Dutch in their encounters with the tides.

There has been some fault in the Dutch, making them subject to the slight derision of the nations who hold themselves to be more romantic, and, as it were, more slender. We English, once upon a time, did especially flout the little nation then acting a history that proved worth the writing. It may be no more than a brief perversity that has set a number of our writers to cheer the memory of Charles II. Perhaps, even, it is no more than another rehearsal of that untiring success at the expense of the bourgeois. To acclaim the immoral monarch was held to be yet another defiance of the bourgeois. The bourgeois would be more simple than, in fact, he is were he to stand up every time to be shocked; but, perhaps, the mere image of his dismay is enough to reward the fancy of those who practise the wanton art. And, when all is done, who performs for any but an imaginary audience? Surely those companies of spectators and of auditors are not the least of the makings of an author. A few men and women he achieves within his books; but others does he create without, and to those figures of all illusion makes the appeal of his art. More candid is the author who has no outer world, but turns that appeal inwards to his own heart. He has at least a living hearer.

This is by the way. Charles II has been cheered; the feat is done, the dismay is imagined with joy. And yet the Merry Monarch's was a dismal time. Plague, fire, the arrears of pension from the French King remembered and claimed by the restored throne of England, and the Dutch in the Medway—all this was disaster. None the less, having the vanity of new clothes and a pretty figure, did we—especially by the mouth of Andrew Marvell—deride our victors, making sport of the Philistines with a proper national sense of enjoyment of such physical disabilities, or such natural difficulties, or such misfavour of fortune, as may beset the alien.

Especially were the denials of fortune matter for English merriment. They are so still; or they were so certainly in the day when a great novelist found the smallness of some South German States to be the subject of unsating banter. The German scenes at the end of "Vanity Fair," for example, may prove how much the ridicule of mere smallness, fewness, poverty, rejoiced the sense of humour in a writer and moralist who thought that he meant to teach mankind to be less worldly. In Andrew Marvell's day they were even more candid. The poverty of privation itself was provocative of the sincere laughter of the inmost man, the true, infrequent laughter of the heart. Marvell, the Puritan, laughed that very laughter—at leanness, at hunger, cold, and solitude—in one memorable satire. I speak of "Flecno, an English Priest in Rome," wherein nothing is spared—not the smallness of the lodging, nor the lack of a bed, nor the scantiness of clothing, nor the fast.

This basso-rilievo of a man—

personal meagreness is the first joke and the last.

It is not then to be wondered at that Marvell should find in the smallness of the country of Holland matter for a cordial jest. But, besides the smallness, there was that accidental and natural disadvantage in regard to the sea. In the Venetians, commerce with the sea, conflict with the sea, a victory over the sea, and the ensuing peace—albeit a less instant battle and a more languid victory—were confessed to be noble; in the Dutch they were grotesque. "With mad labour," says Andrew Marvell, with the spirited consciousness of the citizen of a country well above ground and free to watch the labour at leisure, "with mad labour" did the Dutch "fish the land to shore."

> How did they rivet with gigantic piles,
> Thorough the centre, their new-catched miles,
> And to the stake a struggling country bound,
> Where barking waves still bait the forced ground;
> Building their watery Babel far more high
> To reach the sea than those to scale the sky!

It is done with a jolly wit, and in what admirable couplets!

> The fish oft-times the burgher dispossessed,
> And sat, not as a meat, but as a guest.

And it is even better sport that the astonished tritons and sea-nymphs should find themselves provided with a capital *cabillau* of shoals of pickled Dutchmen (heeren for herring, says Marvell); and it must be allowed that he rhymes with the enjoyment of irony. There is not a smile for us in " Flecno," but it is more than possible to smile over this " Character of Holland "; at the excluded ocean returning to play at leap-frog over the steeples; at the rise of government and authority in Holland, which belonged of right to the man who could best invent a shovel or a pump, the country being so leaky:

> Not who first sees the rising sun commands,
> But who could first discern the rising lands.

We have lost something more than the delighted laughter of Marvell, more than his practical joke, and more than the heart that was light in so burly a frame —we have lost with these the wild humour that wore so well the bonds of two equal lines, and was wild with so much order, invention, malice, gaiety, polish, equilibrium, and vitality—in a word, the Couplet, the couplet of the past. We who cannot stand firm within two lines, but must slip beyond and between the boundaries, who tolerate the couplets of Keats and imitate them, should praise the day of Charles II because of Marvell's art, and not for love of the sorry reign. We had plague, fire, and the Dutch in the Medway, but we had the couplet wherewith to make light of our enemies.

It was against a seaport fortress, profoundly walled, that some remembered winter storms lately turned their great artillery. It was a time of resounding nights; the sky was so clamorous and so close, up in the towers of the stronghold, that one seemed to be indeed admitted

to the perturbed counsels of the winds. The gale came
with an indescribable haste, hooting as it flew; it
seemed to break itself upon the heights, yet passed
unbroken out to sea; in the voice of the sea there were
pauses, but none in that of the urgent gale with its
hoo-hoo-hoo all night, that clamoured down the calling of the waves. That lack of pauses was the strangest
thing in the tempest, because the increase of sound
seemed to imply a lull before. The lull was never perceptible, but the lift was always an alarm. The on-
slaught was instant, where would it stop? What was
the secret extreme to which this hurry and force were
tending? You asked less what thing was driving the
flocks of the storm than what was calling them. And
there were moments when the end seemed about to be
attained.

The wind struck us hasty blows, and unawares we
borrowed, to describe it, words fit for the sharp strokes
of material things; but the fierce gale is soft. Along
the short grass, trembling and cowering flat on the
scarped hill-side, against the staggering horse, against
the flint walls, one with the rock they grasp, the bat-
tery of the tempest is a quick and enormous softness.
What down, what sand, what deep moss, what elastic
wave could match the bed and cushion of the gale?

This storm tossed the wave and the stones of the
sea-wall up together. The next day it left the waters
white with the thrilling whiteness of foam in sunshine.
It was only the Channel; and in such narrow waters
you do not see the distances, the wide levels of fleeting
and floating foam, that lie light between long wave and
long wave on a Mediterranean coast, regions of delicate

and transitory brightness so far out that all the waves,
near and far, seemed to be breaking at the same moment, one beyond the other, and league beyond league,
into foam. But the Channel has its own strong, short
curl that catches the rushing shingle up with the freshest of all noises and runs up with sudden curves,
white upon the white sea-wall, under the
random shadow of sea-gulls and the
light of a shining cloud.

ARTS

TITHONUS

"IT was resolved," said the morning paper, "to colour the borders of the panels and other spaces of Portland stone with arabesques and other patterns, but that no paint should be used, as paint would need renewing from time to time. The colours, therefore," —and here is the passage to be noted—"are all mixed with wax liquefied with petroleum; and the wax surface sets as hard as marble. . . . The wax is left time to form an imperishable surface of ornament, which would have to be cut out of the stone with a chisel if it was desired to remove it." Not, apparently, that a new surface is formed which, by much violence and perseverance, could, years hence, be chipped off again; but that the "ornament" is driven in and incorporate, burnt in and absorbed, so that there is nothing possible to cut away by any industry. In this humorous form of ornament we are beforehand with Posterity. Posterity is baffled.

Will this victory over our sons' sons be the last resolute tyranny prepared by one age for the coercion, constraint, and defeat of the future? To impose that compulsion has been hitherto one of the strongest of human desires. It is one, doubtless, to be outgrown by the human race; but how slowly that growth creeps onwards, let the success in the stencilling of St. Paul's teach us, to our confusion. There is evidently a man

—a group of men—happy at this moment because it has been possible, by great ingenuity, to force our posterity to have their cupola of St. Paul's with the stone mouldings stencilled and "picked out" with niggling colours, whether that undefended posterity like it or not. And this is a survival of one of the obscure pleasures of man, attested by history.

It is impossible to read the Thirty-nine Articles, for example, and not to recognize in those acts of final, all-resolute, eager, eternal legislation one of the strongest of all recorded proofs of this former human wish. If Galileo's Inquisitors put a check upon the earth, which yet moved, a far bolder enterprise was the Reformers' who arrested the moving man, and inhibited the moving God. The sixteenth century and a certain part of the age immediately following seem to be times when the desire had conspicuously become a passion. Say the middle of the sixteenth century in Italy and the beginning of the seventeenth in England—for in those days we were somewhat in the rear. *There* is the obstinate, confident, unreluctant, undoubting, and re-solved seizure upon power. *Then* was Rome rebuilt, re-faced, marked with a single sign and style. Then was many a human hand stretched forth to grasp the fate of the unborn. The fortunes and the thoughts of the day to come were to be as the day then present would have them, if the dead hand—the living hand that was then to die, and was to keep its hold in death —could by any means make them fast.

Obviously, to build at all is to impose something upon an age that may be more than willing to build for itself. The day may soon come when no man will do even so much without some impulse of apology. Posterity is not compelled to keep our pictures or our books in existence, nor to read nor to look at them; but it is more or less obliged to have a stone building in view for an age or two. We can hardly avoid some of the forms of tyranny over the future, but few, few are the living men who would consent to share in this ingenuity at St. Paul's—this petroleum and this wax.

In 1842 they were discussing the decoration of the Houses of Parliament, and the efforts of all in council were directed upon the future. How the frescoes then to be achieved by the artists of the day should be made secure against all mischances—smoke, damp, " the risk of bulging," even accidents attending the washing of upper floors—all was discussed in confidence with the public. It was impossible for anyone who read the papers then to escape from some at least of the responsibilities of technical knowledge. From Genoa, from Rome, from Munich especially, all kinds of expert and most deliberate schemes were gathered in order to defeat the natural and not superfluous operation of efficient and effacing time.

The academic little capital of Bavaria had, at about the same date, decorated a vast quantity of wall space of more than one order of architecture. Art revived and was encouraged at that time and place with unparalleled obstinacy. They had not the malice of the petroleum that does violence to St. Paul's; but they had instead an indomitable patience. Under the commands of the master Cornelius, they baffled time and all his work—refused his pardons, his absolutions, his cancelling indulgences—by a perseverance that nothing

could discourage. Who has not known somewhat indifferent painters mighty busy about their colours and
varnishes? Cornelius caused a pit to be dug for the
preparation of the lime, and in the case of the Ludwig
Kirche this lime remained there for eight years, with
frequent stirrings. This was in order that the whole
fresco, when at last it was entrusted to its bed, should
be set there for immortality. Nor did the master fail
to thwart time by those mechanical means that should
avert the risk of bulging already mentioned. He neglected no detail. He was provident, and he lay in wait
for more than one of the laws of nature, to frustrate
them. Gravitation found him prepared, and so did the
less majestic but not vain dispensation of accidents.
Against bulging he had an underplot of tiles set on
end; against possible trickling from an upper floor he
had asphalt; it was all part of the human conspiracy.
In effect, the dull pictures at Munich seem to stand
well. It would have been more just—so the present
age thinks of these preserved walls—if the day that
admired them had had them exclusively, and our day
had been exempt. The painted cathedrals of the
Middle Ages have undergone the natural correction;
why not the Ludwig Kirche?

In 1842, then, the nations were standing, as it were,
shoulder to shoulder against the walk of time and
against his gentle act and art. They had just called
iron into their cabal. Cornelius came from Munich to
London, looked at the walls at Westminster, and put
a heart of confidence into the breast of the Com-
mission. The situation, he averred, need not be too
damp for immortality, with due care. What he had

done in the Glyptothek and in the Pinacothek might be done with the best results in England, in defiance of the weather, of the river, of the mere days, of the divine order of alteration, and, in a word, of heaven and earth.

Meanwhile, there was that good servant of the law of change, lime that had not been kept quite long enough, ready to fulfil its mission; they would have none of it. They evaded it, studied its ways, and put it to the rout. "Many failures that might have been hastily attributed to damp were really owing to the use of lime in too fresh a state. Of the experimental works painted at Munich, those only have faded which are known to have been done without due attention to the materials. *Thus, a figure of Bavaria, painted by Kaulbach, which has faded considerably, is known to have been executed with lime that was too fresh.*" One cannot refrain from italics: the way was so easy; it was only to take a little less of this importunate care about the lime, to have a better confidence, to be more impatient and eager, and all had been well: *not* to do—a virtue of omission.

This is not a matter of art-criticism. It is an ethical question hitherto unstudied. The makers of laws have not always been obliged to face it, inasmuch as their laws are made in part for the present, and in part for that future whereof the present needs to be assured— that is, the future is bound as a guaranty for present security of person or property. Some such hold upon the time to come we are obliged to claim, and to claim it for our own sakes—because of the reflex effect upon our own affairs, and not for the pleasure of fettering the time to come. Every maker of a will does at least this.

Were the men of the sixteenth century so moderate? Not they. They found the present all too narrow for the imposition of their will. It did not satisfy them to disinter and scatter the bones of the dead, nor to efface the records of a past that offended them. It did not satisfy them to bind the present to obedience by imperative menace and instant compulsion. When they had burnt libraries and thrown down monuments and pursued the rebels of the past into the other world, and had seen to it than none living should evade them, then they outraged the future.

Whatever misgivings may have visited those dominant minds as to the effectual and final success of their measures—would their writ run in time as well as place, and were the nameless populations indeed their subjects?—whatever questions may have peered in upon those rigid counsels and upon those busy vigils of the keepers of the world, they silenced by legislation and yet more legislation. They wrote in statute books; they would have written their will across the skies. Their hearts would have burnt for lack of records more inveterate, and of testimonies that mankind should lack courage to question, if in truth they did ever doubt lest posterity might try their lock. Perhaps they did never so much as foresee the race of the unnumbered and emancipated for whom their prohibitions and penalties are no more than documents of history.

If the tyrannous day of our fathers had but possessed the means of these our more diffident times! They, who would have written their present and actual will upon the skies, might certainly have written in petroleum and wax upon the stone. Fate did them wrong in withholding from their hands this means of finality and violence. Into our hands it has been given at a time when the student of the race thought, perhaps, that we had been proved in the school of forbearance. Something, indeed, we may have learnt therein, but not enough, as we now find.

We have not yet the natural respect for the certain knowledge and the probable wisdom of our successors. A certain reverend official document, not guiltless of some confusion of thought, lately recommended to the veneration of the present times " those past ages with their store of experience." Doubtless, as the posterity of their predecessors our predecessors had experience, but, as our ancestors, none—none. Therefore, if they were a little reverend our own posterity is quite reverend. It is a flippant and novelty-loving humour that so flatters the unproved past and refuses the deference due to the burden of years which is ours, which—grown still graver—will be our children's.

SYMMETRY AND INCIDENT

THE art of Japan has none but an exterior part in the history of the art of nations. Being in its own methods and attitude the art of accident, it has, appropriately, an accidental value. It is of accidental value, and not of integral necessity. The virtual discovery of Japanese art, during the middle years of the second French Empire, caused Europe to relearn how expedient, how delicate, and how lovely Incident may look when Symmetry has grown vulgar. The lesson was most welcome. Japan has had her full influence. European art has learnt the value of position and the tact of the unique. But Japan is unlessoned, and (in all her characteristic art) content with her own conventions; she is local, provincial, alien, remote, incapable of equal companionship with a world that has Greek art in its own history—Pericles " to its father."

Nor is it pictorial art, or decorative art only, that has been touched by Japanese example of Incident and the Unique. Music had attained the noblest form of symmetry in the eighteenth century, but in music, too, symmetry had since grown dull; and momentary music, the music of phase and of fragment, succeeded. The sense of symmetry is strong in a complete melody—of symmetry in its most delicate and lively and least stationary form—balance; whereas the *leit-motif* is isolated. In domestic architecture Symmetry and In-

cident make a familiar antithesis—the very commonplace of rival methods of art. But the same antithesis
exists in less obvious forms. The poets have sought
"irregular" metres. Incident hovers, in the very act
of choosing its right place, in modern, or recent,
portraiture. In this we have, if not the Japanese
suppression of minor emphasis, certainly the Japanese
exaggeration of major emphasis; and with this a quick-
ness and buoyancy. The smile, the figure, the drapery
—not yet settled from the arranging touch of a hand,
and showing its mark—the restless and unstationary
foot, and the unity of impulse that has passed everywhere like a single breeze, all these have a life that
greatly transcends the life of Japanese art, yet has the
light touch of Japanese incident. In passing, a charming comparison may be made between such portraiture
and the aspect of an aspen or other tree of light and
liberal leaf; whether still or in motion the aspen and
the free-leafed poplar have the alertness and expectancy
of flight in all their flocks of leaves, while the oaks and
elms are gathered in their station. All this is not Japanese, but from such accident is Japanese art inspired,
with its good luck of perceptiveness.

What symmetry is to form, that is repetition in the
art of ornament. Greek art and Gothic alike have
series, with repetition or counterchange for their ruling
motive. It is hardly necessary to draw the distinction
between this motive and that of the Japanese. The
Japanese motives may be defined as uniqueness and
position. And these were not known as motives of
decoration before the study of Japanese decoration.
Repetition and counterchange, of course, have their

place in Japanese ornament, as in the diaper patterns for which these people have so singular an invention, but here, too, uniqueness and position are the principal inspiration. And it is quite worth while, and much to the present purpose, to call attention to the chief peculiarity of the Japanese diaper patterns, which is *interruption*. Repetition there must necessarily be in these, but symmetry is avoided by an interruption which is, to the Western eye, at least, perpetually and freshly unexpected. The place of the interruptions of lines, the variation of the place, and the avoidance of correspondence, are precisely what makes Japanese design of this class inimitable. Thus, even in a repeating pattern, you have a curiously successful effect of impulse. It is as though a separate intention had been formed by the designer at every angle. Such renewed consciousness does not make for greatness. Greatness in design has more peace than is found in the gentle abruptness of Japanese lines, in their curious brevity. It is scarcely necessary to say that a line, in all other schools of art, is long or short according to its place and purpose; but only the Japanese designer so contrives his patterns that the line is always short; and many repeating designs are entirely composed of this various and variously-occurring brevity, this prankish avoidance of the goal. Moreover, the Japanese evade symmetry, in the unit of their repeating patterns, by another simple device—that of numbers. They make a small difference in the number of curves and of lines. A great difference would not make the same effect of variety; it would look too much like a contrast. For example, three rods on one side and six on another would be

something else than a mere variation, and variety would
be lost by the use of them. The Japanese decorator
will vary three in this place by two in that, and a sense
of the defeat of symmetry is immediately produced.
With more violent means the idea of symmetry would
have been neither suggested nor refuted.

Leaving mere repeating patterns and diaper designs,
you find, in Japanese compositions, complete designs in
which there is no point of symmetry. It is a balance of
suspension and of antithesis. There is no sense of lack
of equilibrium, because place is, most subtly, made to
have the effect of giving or of subtracting value. A
small thing is arranged to reply to a large one, for the
small thing is placed at the precise distance that makes
it a (Japanese) equivalent. In Italy (and perhaps in
other countries) the scales commonly in use are furnished with only a single weight that increases or
diminishes in value according as you slide it nearer or
further upon a horizontal arm. It is equivalent to so
many ounces when it is close to the upright, and to so
many pounds when it hangs from the farther end of
the horizontal rod. Distance plays some such part
with the twig or the bird in the upper corner of a
Japanese composition. Its place is its significance and
its value. Such an art of position implies a great art of
intervals. The Japanese chooses a few things and
leaves the space between them free, as free as the pauses
or silences in music. But as time, not silence, is the
subject, or material, of contrast in musical pauses, so
it is the measurement of space—that is, collocation—
that makes the value of empty intervals. The space
between this form and that, in a Japanese composition,

is valuable because it is just so wide and no more. And this, again, is only another way of saying that position is the principle of this apparently wilful art.

Moreover, the alien art of Japan, in its pictorial form, has helped to justify the more stenographic school of etching. Greatly transcending Japanese expression, the modern etcher has undoubtedly accepted moral support from the islands of the Japanese. He too etches a kind of shorthand, even though his notes appeal much to the spectator's knowledge, while the Oriental shorthand appeals to nothing but the spectator's simple vision. Thus the two artists work in ways dissimilar. Nevertheless, the French etcher would never have written his signs so freely had not the Japanese so freely drawn his own. Furthermore still, the transitory and destructible material of Japanese art has done as much as the multiplication of newspapers, and the discovery of processes, to reconcile the European designer—the black and white artist—to working for the day, the day of publication. Japan lives much of its daily life by means of paper, painted; so does Europe by means of paper, printed. But as we, unlike those Orientals, are a destructive people, paper with us means short life, quick abolition, transformation, re-appearance, a very circulation of life. This is our present way of surviving ourselves—the new version of that feat of life. Time was when to survive yourself meant to secure, for a time indefinitely longer than the life of man, such dull form as you had given to your work; to intrude upon posterity. To survive yourself, to-day, is to let your work go into daily oblivion.

Now, though the Japanese are not a destructive people,

their paper does not last for ever, and that material has clearly suggested to them a different condition of ornament from that with which they adorned old lacquer, fine ivory, or other perdurable things. For the transitory material they keep the more purely pictorial art of landscape. What of Japanese landscape? Assuredly it is too far reduced to a monotonous convention to merit serious study by races that have produced Cotman and Corot. Japanese landscape-drawing reduces things seen to such fewness as must have made the art insufferably tedious to any people less fresh-spirited and more inclined to take themselves seriously than these Orientals. A preoccupied people would never endure it. But a little closer attention from the Occidental student might find for the evasive attitude towards landscape—it is an attitude almost traitorously evasive —a more significant reason. It is that the distances, the greatness, the winds and the waves of the world, coloured plains, and the flight of a sky, are all certainly alien to the perceptions of a people intent upon little deformities. Does it seem harsh to define by that phrase the curious Japanese search for accidents? Upon such search these people are avowedly intent, even though they show themselves capable of exquisite appreciation of the form of a normal bird and of the habit of growth of a normal flower. They are not in search of the perpetual slight novelty which was Aristotle's ideal of the language poetic (" a little wildly, or with the flower of the mind," says Emerson of the way of a poet's speech)—and such novelty it is, like the frequent pulse of the pinion, that keeps verse upon the wing; no, what the Japanese are intent upon is perpetual slight

disorder. In Japan the man in the fields has eyes less
for the sky and the crescent moon than for some stone
in the path, of which the asymmetry strikes his curious
sense of pleasure in fortunate accident of form. For
love of a little grotesque strangeness he will load himself with the stone and carry it home to his garden.
The art of such a people is not liberal art, not the art
of peace, and not the art of humanity. Look at the
curls and curves whereby this people conventionally
signify wave or cloud. All these curls have an attitude which is like that of a figure slightly malformed,
and not like that of a human body that is perfect,
dominant, and if bent, bent at no lowly or niggling
labour. Why these curves should be so charming it
would be hard to say; they have an exquisite prankish-
ness of variety, the place where the upward or downward scrolls curl off from the main wave is delicately
unexpected every time, and—especially in gold em-
broideries—is sensitively fit for the material, catching
and losing the light, while the lengths of waving line
are such as the long gold threads take by nature.

A moment ago this art was declared not human.
And, in fact, in no other art has the figure suffered
such crooked handling. The Japanese have generally
evaded even the local beauty of their own race for the
sake of perpetual slight deformity. Their beauty is
remote from our sympathy and admiration; and it is
quite possible that we might miss it in pictorial pre-
sentation, and that the Japanese artist may have intended human beauty where we do not recognize it.
But if it is not easy to recognize, it is certainly not
difficult to guess at. And, accordingly, you are gener-

ally aware that the separate beauty of the race, and its separate dignity, even—to be very generous—has been admired by the Japanese artist, and is represented here and there occasionally, in the figure of warrior or mousmé. But even with this exception the habit of Japanese figure-drawing is evidently grotesque, derisive, and crooked. It is curious to observe that the search for slight deformity is so constant as to make use, for its purposes, not of action only, but of perspective foreshortening. With us it is to the youngest child only that there would appear to be mirth in the drawing of a man who, stooping violently forward, would seem to have his head " beneath his shoulders." The European child would not see fun in the living man so presented, but— unused to the same effect " in the flat "—he thinks it ,prodigiously humorous in a drawing. But so only when he is quite young. The Japanese keeps, apparently, his sense of this kind of humour. It amuses him, but not perhaps altogether as it amuses the child, that the foreshortened figure should, in drawing and to the unpractised eye, seem distorted and dislocated; the simple Oriental appears to find more derision in it than the simple child. The distortion is not without a suggestion of ignominy. And, moreover, the Japanese shows derision, but not precisely scorn. He does not hold himself superior to his hideous models. He makes free with them on equal terms. He is familiar with them.

And if this is the conviction gathered from ordinary drawings, no need to insist upon the ignoble character of those that are intentional caricatures.

Perhaps the time has hardly come for writing anew

the praises of symmetry. The world knows too much of the abuse of Greek decoration, and would be glad to forget it, with the intention of learning that art afresh in a future age and of seeing it then anew. But whatever may be the phases of the arts, there is the abiding principle of symmetry in the body of man, that goes erect, like an upright soul. Its balance is equal. Exterior human symmetry is surely a curious physiological fact where there is no symmetry interiorly. For the centres of life and movement within the body are placed with Oriental inequality. Man is Greek without and Japanese within. But the absolute symmetry of the skeleton and of the beauty and life that cover it is accurately a principle. It controls, but not tyrannously, all the life of human action. Attitude and motion disturb perpetually, with infinite incidents— inequalities of work, war, and pastime, inequalities of sleep—the symmetry of man. Only in death and " at attention " (the soldier's) is that symmetry complete in attitude. Nevertheless, it rules the dance and the battle, and its rhythm is not to be destroyed. All the more because this hand holds the goad and that the harrow, this the shield and that the sword, because this hand rocks the cradle and that caresses the unequal heads of children, is this rhythm the law; and grace and strength are inflections thereof. All human movement is a variation upon symmetry, and without symmetry it would not be variation; it would be lawless, fortuitous, and as dull and broadcast as lawless art. The order of in- flection that is not infraction has been explained in a most authoritative sentence of criticism of literature, a sentence that should save the world the trouble of some

of its present futile, violent, and weak experiments:
"Law, the rectitude of humanity," says Coventry
Patmore, "should be the poet's only subject, as, from
time immemorial, it has been the subject of true art,
though many a true artist has done the Muse's will and
knew it not. As all the music of verse arises, not
from infraction but from inflection of the law of the
set metre; so the greatest poets have been those the
modulus of whose verse has been most variously and
delicately inflected, in correspondence with feelings
and passions which are the inflections of moral law in
their theme. Law puts a strain upon feeling, and feeling responds with a strain upon law. Furthermore,
Aristotle says that the quality of poetic language is a
continual *slight* novelty. In the highest poetry, like
that of Milton, these three modes of inflection, metrical,
linguistical, and moral, all chime together in praise of
the truer order of life."

And like that order is the order of the figure of man,
an order most beautiful and most secure when it is put
to the proof. That perpetual proof by perpetual inflection is the very condition of life. Symmetry is a profound, if disregarded because perpetually inflected,
condition of human life.

The nimble art of Japan is unessential; it may come
and go, may settle or be fanned away. It has life and
it is not without law; it has an obvious life, and a less
obvious law. But with Greece abides the obvious law
and the less obvious life: symmetry as apparent as the
symmetry of the form of man, and life occult like his
unequal heart. And this seems to be the nobler and
the more perdurable relation.

THE PLAID

IT is disconcerting to hear of the plaid in India. Our dyes, we know, they use in the silk mills of Bombay, with the deplorable result that their clothes, when they grow old, are dull and unintentionally falsified with infelicitous decay. The Hindus are a washing people; and the sun and water that do but dim, soften, and warm the native vegetable dyes to the last, do but burlesque the aniline. Magenta is bad enough when it is itself; but the worst of magenta is that it spoils but poorly. No bad modern forms and no bad modern colours spoil well. And spoiling is an important process. It is a test—one of the ironical tests that come too late with their proofs. London portico-houses will make some such ruins as do chemical dyes, which undergo no use but derides them, no accidents but caricature them. This is an old enough grievance. But the plaid!

The plaid is the Scotsman's contribution to the decorative art of the world. Scotland has no other indigenous decoration. In his most admirable lecture on " The Two Paths," Ruskin acknowledged, with a passing misgiving, that his Highlanders had little art. And the misgiving was but passing, because he considered how fatally wrong was the art of India—" it never represents a natural fact. It forms its compositions out

of meaningless fragments of colour and flowings of line.
. . . It will not draw a man, but an eight-armed mon-
ster; it will not draw a flower, but only a spiral or a
zig-zag." Because of this aversion from Nature the
Hindu and his art tended to evil, Ruskin tells us. But
of the Scot we are told, " You will find upon reflection
that all the highest points of the Scottish character are
connected with impressions derived straight from the
natural scenery of their country."

What, then, about the plaid? Where is the natural
fact there? If the Indian, by practising a non-natural
art of spirals and zig-zags, cuts himself off " from all
possible sources of healthy knowledge or natural delight," to what did the good and healthy Highlander
condemn himself by practising the art of the plaid? A
spiral may be found in the vine, and a zig-zag in the
lightning, but where in nature is the plaid to be found?
There is surely no curve or curl that can be drawn by
a designing hand but is a play upon some infinitely
various natural fact. The smoke of the cigarette, more
sensitive in motion than breath or blood, has its waves
so multitudinously inflected and reinflected, with such
flights and such delays, it flows and bends upon currents
of so subtle influence and impulse as to include the
most active, impetuous, and lingering curls ever drawn
by the finest Oriental hand—and that is not a Hindu
hand, nor any hand of Aryan race. The Japanese has
captured the curve of the section of a sea-wave—its
flow, relaxation, and fall; but this is a single movement, whereas the line of cigarette-smoke in a still
room fluctuates in twenty delicate directions. No, it is
impossible to accept the saying that the poor spiral or

scroll of a human design is anything but a participation in the innumerable curves and curls of nature.

Now the plaid is not only "cut off" from natural sources, as Ruskin says of Oriental design—the plaid is not only cut off from nature, and cut off from nature by the yard (for it is to be measured off in inorganic quantity); but it is even a kind of intentional contradiction of all natural or vital forms. And it is equally defiant of vital tone and of vital colour. Everywhere in nature tone is gradual, and between the fainting of a tone and the failing of a curve there is a charming analogy. But the tartan insists that its tone shall be invariable, and sharply defined by contrasts of dark and light. As to colour, it has colours, not colour.

But that plaid should now go so far afield as to decorate the noble garment of the Indies is ill news. True, Ruskin saw nothing but cruelty and corruption in Indian life or art; but let us hear an Indian maxim in regard to those who, in cruel places, are the readiest sufferers: "There," says the "Mahabharata," "where women are treated with respect, the very gods are said to be filled with joy. Women deserve to be honoured. Serve ye them. Bend your will before them. By honouring women ye are sure to attain to the fruition of all things." And the rash teachers of our youth would have persuaded us that this generous lesson was first learnt in Teutonic forests!

Nothing but extreme feminine lowliness can well reply, or would probably be suffered to reply, to this Hindu profession of masculine reverence. Accordingly the woman so honoured makes an offering of cakes and oil to the souls of her mother-in-law, grandmother-in-law, and great grandmother-in-law, in gratitude for their giving her a good husband. And to go back for a moment to Ruskin's contrast of the two races, it was assuredly under the stress of some too rash reasoning that he judged the lovely art of the East as a ministrant to superstition, cruelty, and pleasure, whether wrought upon the temple, the sword, or the girdle. The innocent art of innocent Hindu women for centuries decked their most modest heads, their dedicated and sequestered beauty, their child-loving breasts, and consecrated chambers.

THE FLOWER

THERE is a form of oppression that has not until now been confessed by those who suffer from it or who are participants, as mere witnesses, in its tyranny. It is the obsession of man by the flower. In the shape of the flower his own paltriness revisits him—his triviality, his sloth, his cheapness, his whole-sale habitualness, his slatternly ostentation. These return to him and wreak upon him their dull revenges. What the tyranny really had grown to can be gauged nowhere so well as in country lodgings, where the most ordinary things of design and decoration have sifted down and gathered together, so that foolish ornament gains a cumulative force and achieves a conspicuous commonness. Stem and petal and leaf— the fluent forms that a man has not by heart but certainly by rote—are woven, printed, cast, and stamped wherever restlessness and insimplicity have feared to leave plain spaces. The most ugly of all imaginable rooms, which is probably the parlour of a farm-house arrayed for those whom Americans call summer-boarders, is beset with flowers. It blooms, a dry, woollen, papery, cast-iron garden. The floor flourishes with blossoms adust, poorly conventionalized into a kind of order; the table-cover is ablaze with a more realistic florescence; the wall-paper is set with bunches; the rigid machine-lace curtain is all of roses and lilies

in its very construction; over the muslin blinds an
impotent sprig is scattered. In the worsted rosettes of
the bell-ropes, in the plaster picture-frames, in the
painted tea-tray and on the cups, in the pediment of
the sideboard, in the ornament that crowns the baro-
meter, in the finials of sofa and arm-chair, in the
finger-plates of the " grained " door, is to be seen the
ineffectual portrait or to be traced the stale inspiration
of the flower. And what is this bossiness around the
grate but some blunt, black-leaded garland? The recital is wearisome, but the retribution of the flower is
precisely weariness. It is the persecution of man, the
haunting of his trivial visions, and the oppression of his
inconsiderable brain.

The man so possessed suffers the lot of the weak-
ling—subjection to the smallest of the things he has
abused. The designer of cheap patterns is no more
inevitably ridden by the flower than is the vain and
transitory author by the phrase. In literature as in
all else man merits his subjection to trivialities by his
economical greed. A condition for using justly and
gaily any decoration would seem to be a measure of
reluctance. Ornament—strange as the doctrine sounds
in a world decivilized—was in the beginning intended
to be something jocund; and jocundity was never to
be achieved but by postponement, deference, and
modesty. Nor can the prodigality of the meadows in
May be quoted in dispute. For Nature has something
even more severe than modertion: she has an innumerable singleness. Her buttercup meadows are not
prodigal; they show multitude, but not multiplicity,
and multiplicity is exactly the disgrace of decoration.

Who has ever multiplied or repeated his delights? or
who has ever gained the granting of the most foolish
of his wishes—the prayer for reiteration? It is a
curious slight to generous Fate that man should, like
a child, ask for one thing many times. Her answer
every time is a resembling but new and single gift;
until the day when she shall make the one tremendous
difference among her gifts—and make it perhaps in
secret—by naming one of them the ultimate. What,
for novelty, what, for singleness, what, for separateness, can equal the last? Of many thousand kisses the
poor last—but even the kisses of your mouth are all
numbered.

UNSTABLE EQUILIBRIUM

IT is principally for the sake of the leg that a change
in the dress of man is so much to be desired. The
leg, completing as it does the form of man, should
make a great part of that human scenery which is at
least as important as the scenery of geological structure,
or the scenery of architecture, or the scenery of vege-
tation, but which the lovers of mountains and the
preservers of ancient buildings have consented to
ignore. The leg is the best part of the figure, inasmuch as it has the finest lines and therewith those
slender, diminishing forms which, coming at the base
of the human structure, show it to be a thing of life
by its unstable equilibrium. A lifeless structure is in
stable equilibrium; the body, springing, poised, upon
its fine ankles and narrow feet, never stands without
implying and expressing life. It is the leg that first
suggested the phantasy of flight. We imagine wings
to the figure that is erect upon the vital and tense
legs of man; and the herald Mercury, because of his
station, looks new-lighted. All this is true of the best
leg, and the best leg is the man's. That of the young
child, in which the Italian schools of painting delighted, has neither movement nor supporting strength.
In the case of the woman's figure it is the foot, with
its extreme proportional smallness, that gives the
precious instability, the spring and balance that are so

organic. But man should no longer disguise the long lines, the strong forms, in those lengths of piping or tubing that are of all garments the most stupid. Inexpressive of what they clothe as no kind of concealing drapery could ever be, they are neither implicitly nor explicitly good raiment. It is hardly possible to err by violence in denouncing them. Why, when an indifferent writer is praised for "clothing his thought," it is to modern raiment that one's agile fancy flies—fain of completing the metaphor!

The human scenery: yes, costume could make a crowd something other than the mass of sooty colour —dark without depth—and the multiplication of undignified forms that fill the streets, and demonstrate, and meet, and listen to the speaker. For the undistinguished are very important by their numbers. These are they who make the look of the artificial world. They are man generalized; as units they inevitably lack something of interest; all the more they have cumulative effect. It would be well if we could persuade the average man to take on a certain human dignity in the clothing of his average body. Unfortunately he will be slow to be changed. And as to the poorer part of the mass, so wretched are their national customs—and the wretchedest of them all the wearing of other men's old raiment—that they must wait for reform until the reformed dress, which the reformers have not yet put on, shall have turned second-hand.

VICTORIAN CARICATURE

THERE has been no denunciation, and perhaps even no recognition, of a certain social immorality in the caricature of the mid-century and earlier. Literary and pictorial alike, it had for its aim the vulgarizing of the married woman. No one now would read Douglas Jerrold for pleasure, but it is worth while to turn up that humourist's serial, "Mrs. Caudle's Curtain Lectures," which were presumably considered good comic reading in the "Punch" of that time, and to make acquaintance with a certain ideal of the grotesque. Obviously to make a serious comment on anything which others consider or have considered humorous is to put oneself at a disadvantage. He who sees the joke holds himself somewhat the superior of the man who would see it, such as it is, if he thought it worth his eyesight. The last-named has to bear the least tolerable of modern reproaches—that he lacks humour; but he need not always care. Now to turn over Douglas Jerrold's monologues is to find that people in the mid-century took their mirth principally from the life of the *arrière boutique*. On that shabby stage was enacted the comedy of literature. Therefore we must take something of the vulgarity of Jerrold as a circumstance of the social ranks wherein he delighted. But the essential vulgarity is that of the woman. There is in some old "Punch" volume

a drawing by Leech—whom one is weary of hearing
named the gentle, the refined—where the work of
the artist has vied with the spirit of the letterpress.
Douglas Jerrold treats of the woman's jealousy, Leech
of her stays. They lie on a chair by the bed, beyond
description gross. And page by page the woman is
derided, with an unfailing enjoyment of her foolish
ugliness of person, of manners, and of language. In
that time there was, moreover, one great humourist,
one whom I infinitely admire; he, too, I am grieved to
remember, bore his part willingly in vulgarizing the
woman; and the part that fell to him was the vulgarizing of the act of maternity. Woman spiteful, woman
suing man at the law for evading her fatuous companionship, woman incoherent, woman abandoned without restraint to violence and temper, woman feigning
sensibility—in none of these ignominies is woman so
common and so foolish for Dickens as she is in child-
bearing.

I named Leech but now. He was, in all things
essential, Dickens's contemporary. And accordingly
the married woman and her child are humiliated by his
pencil; not grossly, but commonly. For him she is
moderately and dully ridiculous. What delights him as
humorous is that her husband—himself wearisome
enough to die of—is weary of her, finds the time long,
and tries to escape her. It amuses him that she should
furtively spend money over her own dowdiness, to the
annoyance of her husband, and that her husband should
have no desire to adorn her, and that her mother should
be intolerable. It pleases him that her baby, with
enormous cheeks and a hideous rosette in its hat—a

burlesque baby—should be a grotesque object of her love, for that too makes subtly for her abasement. Charles Keene, again—another contemporary, though he lived into a later and different time. He saw little else than common forms of human ignominy—in-dignities of civic physique, of stupid prosperity, of dress, of bearing. He transmits these things in greater proportion than he found them—whether for love of the humour of them, or by a kind of inverted disgust that is as eager as delight—one is not sure which is the impulse. The grossness of the vulgarities is rendered with a completeness that goes far to convince us of a certain sensitiveness of apprehension in the designer; and then again we get convinced that real apprehension —real apprehensiveness—would not have insisted upon such things, could not have lived with them through almost a whole career. There is one drawing in the "Punch" of years ago, in which Charles Keene achieved the nastiest thing possible to even the inven-tion of that day. A drunken citizen, in the usual broadcloth, has gone to bed, fully dressed, with his boots on and his umbrella open, and the joke lies in the surprise awaiting, when she awakes, the wife asleep at his side in a night-cap. Every one who knows Keene's work can imagine how the huge well-fed figure was drawn, and how the coat wrinkled across the back, and how the bourgeois whiskers were indicated. This obscene drawing is matched by many equally odious. Abject domesticity, ignominies of married life, of middle-age, of money-making; the old common jape against the mother-in-law; abominable weddings: in one drawing a bridegroom with shambling side-long legs asks his bride if she is nervous; she is a widow, and she answers, "No, never was." In all these things there is very little humour. Where Keene achieved fun was in the figures of his schoolboys. The hint of tenderness which in really fine work could never be absent from a man's thought of a child or from his touch of one, however frolic or rowdy the subject in hand, is absolutely lacking in Keene's designs; nevertheless, we acknowledge that there is humour. It is also in some of his clerical figures when they are not caricatures, and certainly in "Robert," the City waiter of "Punch." But so irresistible is the derision of the woman that all Charles Keene's persistent sense of vulgarity is intent centrally upon her. Never for any grace gone astray is she bantered, never for the social extravagances, for prattle, or for beloved dress; but always for her jealousy, and for the repulsive person of the man upon whom she spies and in whom she vindicates her ignoble rights. If this is the shopkeeper the possession of whom is her boast, what then is she?

This great immorality, centring in the irreproachable days of the Exhibition of 1851, or thereabouts—the pleasure in this particular form of human disgrace —has passed, leaving one trace only: the habit by which some men reproach a silly woman through her sex, whereas a silly man is not reproached through his sex. But the vulgarity of which I have written here was distinctively English—the most English thing that England had in days when she bragged of many another —and it was not able to survive an increased commerce of manners and letters with France. It was the chief immorality destroyed by the French novel.

THE POINT OF HONOUR

NOT without significance is the Spanish nation- ality of Velasquez. In Spain was the Point put upon Honour; and Velasquez was the first Impressionist. As an Impressionist he claimed, implicitly if not explicitly, a whole series of delicate trusts in his trustworthiness; he made an appeal to the confidence of his peers; he relied on his own candour, and asked that the candid should rely upon him; he kept the chastity of art when other masters were content with its honesty, and when others saved artistic conscience he safeguarded the point of honour. Contemporary masters more or less proved their position, and convinced the world by something of demonstration; the first Impressionist simply asked that his word should be accepted. To those who would not take his word he offers no bond. To those who will, he grants the distinction of a share in his responsibility.

Somewhat unrefined, in comparison with his lofty and simple claim to be believed on a suggestion, is the commoner painter's production of his credentials, his appeal to the sanctions of ordinary experience, his self-defence against the suspicion of making irresponsible mysteries in art. "You can see for yourself," the lesser man seems to say to the world, "thus things are, and I render them in such manner that your intelligence may be satisfied." This is an appeal to average experience—at the best the cumulative experience; and with the average, or with the sum, art cannot deal without derogation. The Spaniard seems to say: "Thus things are in my pictorial sight. Trust me, I apprehend them so." We are not excluded from his counsels, but we are asked to attribute a certain authority to him, master of the craft as he is, master of that art of seeing pictorially which is the beginning and not far from the end—not far short of the whole—of the art of painting. So little indeed are we shut out from the mysteries of a great Impressionist's impression that Velasquez requires us to be in some degree his colleagues. Thus may each of us to whom he appeals take praise from the praised: he leaves my educated eyes to do a little of the work. He respects my responsibility no less—though he respects it less explicitly—than I do his. What he allows me would not be granted by a meaner master. If he does not hold himself bound to prove his own truth, he returns thanks for my trust. It is as though he used his countrymen's courteous hyperbole and called his house my own. In a sense of the most noble hostship he does me the honours of his picture.

Because Impressionism with all its extreme—let us hope its ultimate—derivatives is so free, therefore is it doubly bound. Because there is none to arraign it, it is a thousand times responsible. To undertake this art for the sake of its privileges without confessing its obligations—or at least without confessing them up to the point of honour—is to take a vulgar freedom: to see immunities precisely where there are duties, and an advantage where there is a bond. A very mob of men have taken Impressionism upon themselves, in several

forms and under a succession of names, in this our
later day. It is against all probabilities that more than
a few among these have within them the point of
honour. In their galleries we are beset with a dim
distrust, And to distrust is more humiliating than to
be distrusted. How many of these landscape-painters,
deliberately rash, are painting the truth of their own
impressions? An ethical question as to loyalty is easily
answered; truth and falsehood as to fact are, happily
for the intelligence of the common conscience, not
hard to divide. But when the *dubium* concerns not
fact but artistic truth, can the many be sure that their
sensitiveness, their candour, their scruple, their delicate
equipoise of perceptions, the vigilance of their apprehension, are enough? Now Impressionists have told us
things as to their impressions—as to the effect of things
upon the temperament of this man and upon the mood
of that—which should not be asserted except on the
artistic point of honour. The majority can tell ordinary
truth, but should not trust themselves for truth extraordinary. They can face the general judgement, but
they should hesitate to produce work that appeals to
the last judgement, which is the judgement within.
There is too much reason to divine that a certain
number of those who aspire to differ from the greatest
of masters have no temperaments worth speaking of,
no point of view worth seizing, no vigilance worth
awaiting, no mood worth waylaying. And to be, *de
parti pris,* an Impressionist without these! O Velasquez!
Nor is literature quite free from a like reproach in her
own things. An author, here and there, will make as
though he had a word worth hearing—nay, worth

over-hearing—a word that seeks to withdraw even
while it is uttered; and yet what it seems to dissemble
is all too probably a platitude. But obviously, literature
is not—as is the craft and mystery of painting—so at
the mercy of a half-imposture, so guarded by unprov-
able honour. For the art of painting is reserved that
shadowy risk, that undefined salvation. If the artistic
temperament—tedious word!—with all its grotesque privileges, becomes yet more common
than it is, there will be yet less responsibility; for the point of honour is the
simple secret of the few.

THE COLOUR OF LIFE

THE COLOUR OF LIFE

RED has been praised for its nobility as the colour of life. But the true colour of life is not red. Red is the colour of violence, or of life broken open, edited, and published. Or if red is indeed the colour of life, it is so only on condition that it is not seen. Once fully visible, red is the colour of life violated, and in the act of betrayal and of waste. Red is the secret of life, and not the manifestation thereof. It is one of the things the value of which is secrecy, one of the talents that are to be hidden in a napkin. The true colour of life is the colour of the body, the colour of the covered red, the implicit and not explicit red of the living heart and the pulses. It is the modest colour of the unpublished blood.

So bright, so light, so soft, so mingled, the gentle colour of life is outdone by all the colours of the world. Its very beauty is that it is white, but less white than milk; brown, but less brown than earth; red, but less red than sunset or dawn. It is lucid, but less lucid than the colour of lilies. It has the hint of gold that is in all fine colour; but in our latitudes the hint is almost elusive. Under Sicilian skies, indeed, it is deeper than old ivory; but under the misty blue of the English zenith, and the warm gray of the London horizon, it is as delicately flushed as the paler wild roses, out to their utmost, flat as stars, in the hedges of the end of June.

For months together London does not see the colour of life in any mass. The human face does not give much of it, what with features, and beards, and the shadow of the top-hat and *chapeau melon* of man, and of the veils of woman. Besides, the colour of the face is subject to a thousand injuries and accidents. The popular face of the Londoner has soon lost its gold, its white, and the delicacy of its red and brown. We miss little beauty by the fact that it is never seen freely in great numbers out-of-doors. You get it in some quantity when all the heads of a great indoor meeting are turned at once upon a speaker; but it is only in the open air, needless to say, that the colour of life is in perfection, in the open air, "clothed with the sun," whether the sunshine be golden and direct, or dazzlingly diffused in gray.

The little figure of the London boy it is that has restored to the landscape the human colour of life. He is allowed to come out of all his ignominies, and to take the late colour of the midsummer north-west evening, on the borders of the Serpentine. At the stroke of eight he sheds the slough of nameless colours —all allied to the hues of dust, soot, and fog, which are the colours the world has chosen for the clothing of its boys—and he makes, in his hundreds, a bright and delicate flush between the gray-blue water and the gray-blue sky. Clothed now with the sun, he is crowned by-and-by with twelve stars as he goes to bathe, and the reflection of an early moon is under his feet.

So little stands between a gamin and all the dignities

of Nature. They are so quickly restored. There seems
to be nothing to do, but only a little thing to undo. It
is like the art of Eleonora Duse. The last and most
finished action of her intellect, passion, and knowledge
was, as it were, the flicking away of some insignificant
thing mistaken for art by other actors, some little
obstacle to the way and liberty of Nature.

All the squalor is gone in a moment, kicked off with
the second boot, and the child goes shouting to complete the landscape with the lacking colour of life.
You are inclined to wonder that, even undressed, he
still shouts with a Cockney accent. You half expect
pure vowels and elastic syllables from his restoration,
his spring, his slenderness, his brightness, and his glow.
Old ivory and wild rose in the deepening midsummer
sun, he gives his colours to his world again.

It is easy to replace man, and it will take no great
time, when Nature has lapsed, to replace Nature. It
is always to do, by the happily easy way of doing
nothing. The grass is always ready to grow in the
streets—and no streets could ask for a more charming
finish than your green grass. The gasometer even must
fall to pieces unless it is renewed; but the grass renews
itself. There is nothing so remediable as the work of
modern man—"a thought which is also," as Mr. Peck-
sniff said, "very soothing." And by remediable I
mean, of course, destructible. As the bathing child
shuffles off his garments—they are few, and one brace
suffices him—so the land might always, in reasonable
time. shuffle off its yellow brick and purple slate, and
all the things that collect about railway stations. A
single night almost clears the air of London.

But if the colour of life looks so well in the rather sham scenery of Hyde Park, it looks brilliant and grave indeed on a real sea-coast. To have once seen it there should be enough to make a colourist. O memorable little picture! The sun was gaining colour as it neared setting, and it set not over the sea, but over the land. The sea had the dark and rather stern, but not cold, blue of that aspect—the dark and not the opal tints. The sky was also deep. Everything was very definite, without mystery, and exceedingly simple. The most luminous thing was the shining white of an edge of foam, which did not cease to be white because it was a little golden and a little rosy in the sunshine. It was still the whitest thing imaginable. And the next most luminous thing was the little unclad child, also invested with the sun and the colour of life.

In the case of women, it is of the living and unpublished blood that the violent world has professed to be delicate and ashamed. See the curious history of the political rights of woman under the Revolution. On the scaffold she enjoyed an ungrudged share in the fortunes of party. Political life might be denied her, but that seems a trifle when you consider how generously she was permitted political death. She was to spin and cook for her citizen in the obscurity of her living hours; but to the hour of her death was granted a part in the largest interests, social, national, international. The blood wherewith she should, according to Robespierre, have blushed to be seen or heard in the tribune, was exposed in the public sight unsheltered by her veins.

Against this there was no modesty. Of all privacies,

the last and the innermost—the privacy of death—was never allowed to put obstacles in the way of public action for a public cause. Women might be, and were, duly silenced when, by the mouth of Olympe de Gouges, they claimed a "right to concur in the choice of representatives for the formation of the laws"; but in her person, too, they were liberally allowed to bear political responsibility to the Republic. Olympe de Gouges was guillotined. Robespierre thus made her public and complete amends.

THE HORIZON

TO mount a hill is to lift with you something
lighter and brighter than yourself or than any
meaner burden. You lift the world, you raise the
horizon; you give a signal for the distance to stand up.
It is like the scene in the Vatican when a Cardinal,
with his dramatic Italian hands, bids the kneeling groups
to arise. He does more than bid them. He lifts them,
he gathers them up, far and near, with the upward
gesture of both arms; he takes them to their feet with
the compulsion of his expressive force. ˙Or it is as when
a conductor takes his players to successive heights of
music. You summon the sea, you bring the mountains,
the distances unfold unlooked-for wings and take an
even flight. You are but a man lifting his weight upon
the upward road, but as you climb the circle of the
world goes up to face you.

Not here or there, but with a definite continuity, the
unseen unfolds. This distant hill outsoars that less
distant, but all are on the wing, and the plain raises its
verge. All things follow and wait upon your eyes. You
lift these up, not by the raising of your eyelids, but by
the pilgrimage of your body. " Lift thine eyes to the
mountains." It is then that other mountains lift themselves to your human eyes.

It is the law whereby the eye and the horizon
answer one another that makes the way up a hill so full

of universal movement. All the landscape is on pilgrimage. The town gathers itself closer, and its inner
harbours literally come to light; the headlands repeat
themselves; little cups within the treeless hills open
and show their farms. In the sea are many regions. A
breeze is at play for a mile or two, and the surface is
turned. There are roads and curves in the blue and
in the white. Not a step of your journey up the height
that has not its replies in the steady motion of land
and sea. Things rise together like a flock of many-
feathered birds.

But it is the horizon, more than all else, you have
come in search of; that is your chief companion on
your way. It is to uplift the horizon to the equality
of your sight that you go high. You give it a distance
worthy of the skies. There is no distance, except the
distance in the sky, to be seen from the level earth;
but from the height is to be seen the distance of this
world. The line is sent back into the remoteness of
light, the verge is removed beyond verge, into a distance
that is enormous and minute.

So delicate and so slender is the distant horizon that
nothing less near than Queen Mab and her chariot
can equal its fineness. Here on the edges of the eyelids,
or there on the edges of the world—we know no other
place for things so exquisitely made, so thin, so small
and tender. The touches of her passing, as close as
dreams, or the utmost vanishing of the forest or the
ocean in the white light between the earth and the air;
nothing else is quite so intimate and fine. The extremities of a mountain view have just such tiny touches as
the closeness of closing eyes shut in.

On the horizon is the sweetest light. Elsewhere colour mars the simplicity of light; but there colour is effaced, not as men efface it, by a blur or darkness, but by mere light. The bluest sky disappears on that shining edge; there is not substance enough for colour. The rim of the hill, of the woodland, of the meadow-land, of the sea—let it only be far enough—has the same absorption of colour; and even the dark things drawn upon the bright edges of the sky are lucid, the light is among them, and they are mingled with it. The horizon has its own way of making bright the pencilled figures of forests, which are black but luminous.

On the horizon, moreover, closes the long perspective of the sky. There you perceive that an ordinary sky of clouds—not a thunder sky—is not a wall but the underside of a floor. You see the clouds that repeat each other grow smaller by distance; and you find a new unity in the sky and earth that gather alike the great lines of their designs to the same distant close. There is no longer an alien sky, tossed up in unintelligible heights.

Of all the things that London has forgone, the most to be regretted is the horizon. Not the bark of the trees in its right colour; not the spirit of the growing grass, which has in some way escaped from the parks; not the smell of the earth unmingled with the odour of soot; but rather the mere horizon. No doubt the sun makes a beautiful thing of the London smoke at times, and in some places of the sky; but not there, not where the soft sharp distance ought to shine. To be dull there is to put all relations and comparisons in the wrong, and to make the sky lawless.

A horizon dark with storm is another thing. The weather darkens the line and defines it, or mingles it with the raining cloud; or softly dims it, or blackens it against a gleam of narrow sunshine in the sky. The stormy horizon will take wing, and the sunny. Go high enough, and you can raise the light from beyond the shower, and the shadow from behind the ray. Only the shapeless and lifeless smoke disobeys and defeats the summons of the eyes.

Up at the top of the seaward hill your first thought is one of some compassion for sailors, inasmuch as they see but little of their sea. A child on a mere Channel cliff looks upon spaces and sizes that they cannot see in the Pacific, on the ocean side of the world. Never in the solitude of the blue water, never between the Cape of Good Hope and Cape Horn, never between the Islands and the West, has the seaman seen anything but a little circle of sea. The Ancient Mariner, when he was alone, did but drift through a thousand narrow solitudes. The sailor has nothing but his mast, indeed. And but for his mast he would be isolated in as small a world as that of a traveller through the plains.

A close circlet of waves is the sailor's famous offing. His offing hardly deserves the name of horizon. To hear him you might think something of his offing, but you do not so when you sit down in the centre of it.

As the upspringing of all things at your going up the heights, so steady, so swift, is the subsidence at your descent. The further sea lies away, hill folds down behind hill. The whole upstanding world, with its looks serene and alert, its distant replies, it signals of many miles, its signs and communications of light, gathers down and pauses. This flock of birds which is the mobile landscape wheels and goes to earth. The Cardinal weighs down the audience with his downward hands. Farewell to the most delicate horizon.

IN JULY

ONE has the leisure of July for perceiving all the differences of the green of leaves. It is no longer a difference in degrees of maturity, for all the trees have darkened to their final tone, and stand in their differences of character and not of mere date. Almost all the green is grave, not sad and not dull. It has a darkened and a daily colour, in majestic but not obvious harmony with dark gray skies, and might look, to inconstant eyes, as prosaic after spring as eleven o'clock looks after the dawn.

Gravity is the word—not solemnity as towards evening, nor menace as at night. The daylight trees of July are signs of common beauty, common freshness, and a mystery familiar and abiding as night and day. In childhood we all have a more exalted sense of dawn and summer sunrise than we ever fully retain or quite recover; and also a far higher sensibility for April and April evenings—a heartache for them, which in riper years is gradually and irretrievably consoled.

Not unbeloved is that serious tree, the elm, with its leaf sitting close, unthrilled. Its stature gives it a dark gold head when it looks alone to a late sun. But if one could go by all the woods, across all the old forests that are now meadowlands set with trees, and could walk a county gathering trees of a single kind in the mind, as one walks a garden collecting flowers of a single kind

in the hand, would not the harvest be a harvest of poplars? A veritable passion for poplars is a most intelligible
passion. The eyes do gather them, far and near, on a
whole day's journey. Not one is unperceived, even
though great timber should be passed, and hill-sides
dense and deep with trees. The fancy makes a poplar
day of it. Immediately the country looks alive with
signals; for the poplars everywhere reply to the glance.
The woods may be all various, but the poplars are
separate.

All their many kinds (and aspens, their kin, must be
counted with them) shake themselves perpetually free
of the motionless forest. It is easy to gather them.
Glances sent into the far distance pay them a flash of
recognition of their gentle flashes; and as you journey
you are suddenly aware of them close by. Light and
the breezes are as quick as the eyes of a poplar-lover to
find the willing tree that dances to be seen.

No lurking for them, no reluctance. One could
never make for oneself an oak day so well. The oaks
would wait to be found, and many would be missed from
the gathering. But the poplars are alert enough for a
traveller by express; they have an alarum aloft, and do
not sleep. From within some little grove of other trees
a single poplar makes a slight sign; or a long row of
poplars suddenly sweep the wind. They are salient
everywhere, and full of replies. They are as fresh as
streams.

It is difficult to realize a drought where there are
many poplars. And yet their green is not rich; the
coolest have a colour much mingled with a cloud-gray.
It does but need fresh and simple eyes to recognize

their unfaded life. When the other trees grow dark and keep still, the poplar and the aspen do not darken —or hardly—and the deepest summer will not find a day in which they do not keep awake. No waters are so vigilant, even where a lake is bare to the wind.

When Keats said of his Dian that she fastened up her hair " with fingers cool as aspen leaves," he knew the coolest thing in the world. It is a coolness of colour, as well as of a leaf which the breeze takes on both sides—the greenish and the grayish. The poplar green has no glows, no gold; it is an austere colour, as little rich as the colour of willows, and less silvery than theirs. The sun can hardly gild it; but he can shine between. Poplars and aspens let the sun through with the wind. You may have the sky sprinkled through them in high midsummer, when all the woods are close.

Sending your fancy poplar-gathering, then, you ensnare wild trees, flying with life. No fisher's net ever took such glancing fishes, nor did the net of a constellation's shape ever enclose more vibrating Pleiades.

CLOUD

DURING a part of the year London does not see
the clouds. Not to see the clear sky might seem
her chief loss, but that is shared by the rest of England,
and is, besides, but a slight privation. Not to see the
clear sky is, elsewhere, to see the cloud. But not so in
London. You may go for a week or two at a time,
even though you hold your head up as you walk, and
even though you have windows that really open, and yet
you shall see no whole cloud, or but a single edge, the
fragment of a form.

Guillotine windows never wholly open, but are filled
with a doubled glass towards the sky when you open
them towards the street. They are, therefore, a sure
sign that for all the years when no other windows
were used in London, nobody there cared much for
the sky, or even knew so much as whether there were
a sky.

But the privation of cloud is indeed a graver loss
than the world knows. Terrestrial scenery is much,
but it is not all. Men go in search of it; but the celestial scenery journeys to them; it goes its way round
the world. It has no nation, it costs no weariness, it
knows no bonds. The terrestrial scenery—the tourist's
—is a prisoner compared with this. The tourist's
scenery moves indeed, but only like Wordsworth's

maiden, with earth's diurnal course; it is made as fast
as its own graves. And for its changes it depends upon
the mobility of the skies. The mere green flushing of
its own sap makes only the least of its varieties; for the
greater it must wait upon the visits of the light. Spring
and autumn are inconsiderable events in a landscape
compared with the shadows of a cloud.

The cloud controls the light, and the mountains on
earth appear or fade according to its passage; they wear
so simply, from head to foot, the luminous gray or the
emphatic purple, as the cloud permits, that their own
local colour and their own local season are lost and
cease, effaced before the all-important mood of the
cloud. The sea has no mood except that of the sky and
of its winds. It is the cloud that, holding the sun's rays in
a sheaf as a giant holds a handful of spears, strikes the
horizon, touches the extreme edge with a delicate re-
velation of light, or suddenly puts it out and makes the
foreground shine.

Every one knows the manifest work of the cloud
when it descends and partakes in the landscape obviously, lies half-way across the mountain slope, stoops
to rain heavily upon the lake, and blots out part of the
view by the rough method of standing in front of it.
But its greatest things are done from its own place,
aloft. Thence does it distribute the sun.

Thence does it lock away between the hills and
valleys more mysteries than a poet conceals, but, like
him, not by interception. Thence it writes out and
cancels all the tracery of Monte Rosa, or lets the
pencils of the sun renew them. Thence, hiding nothing, and yet making dark, it sheds deep colour upon

the forest land of Sussex, so that, seen from the hills, all the country is divided between grave blue and graver sunlight.

But the cloud is never so victorious as when it towers above some little landscape of rather paltry interest—a conventional river heavy with water, gardens with their little evergreens, walks, and shrubberies; and thick trees, impervious to the light, touched, as the novelists always have it, with "autumn tints." High over these rises, in the enormous scale of the scenery of clouds, what no man expected—an heroic sky. Few of the things that were ever done upon earth are great enough to be done under such a heaven. It was surely designed for other days; it is for an epic world. Your eyes sweep a thousand miles of cloud. What are the distances of earth to these, and what are the distances of the clear and cloudless sky? The very horizons of the landscape are near, for the round world dips so soon; and the distances of the mere clear sky are unmeasured—you rest upon nothing until you come to a star, and the star itself is immeasurable.

The cloud, moreover, controls the sun, not merely by keeping the custody of his rays, but by becoming the counsellor of his temper. The cloud veils an angry sun, or, more terribly, lets fly an angry ray, suddenly bright upon tree and tower, with iron-gray storm for a background. Or when anger had but threatened, the cloud reveals him, gentle 'beyond hope. It is in the confidence of the winds, and wears their colours. There is a heavenly game, on south-west wind days, when the clouds are bowled by a breeze from behind the evening. They are round and brilliant, and come leaping

up from the horizon for hours. This is a frolic and
haphazard sky.

All unlike this is the sky that has a centre, and
stands composed about it. As the clouds marshalled
the earthly mountains, so the clouds in turn are now
ranged. The tops of all the celestial Andes aloft are
swept at once by a single ray, warmed with a single
colour. Promontory after league-long promontory of a
stiller Mediterranean in the sky is called out of mist
and gray by the same finger. The cloudland is very
great, but a sunbeam makes all its nations and con-
tinents sudden with light.

The cloud has a name suggesting darkness; nevertheless, it is not merely the guardian of the sun's rays and
their director. It is the sun's treasurer; it holds the
light that the world has lost. We talk of sunshine and
moonshine, but not of cloud-shine, which is yet one
of the illuminations of our skies. A shining cloud is
one of the most majestic of all secondary lights. If
the reflecting moon is the bride, this is "the friend
of the bridegroom."

SHADOWS

ANOTHER good reason why we ought to leave blank, unvexed, and unencumbered with paper patterns the ceiling and walls of a simple house is that the plain surface may be visited by the unique designs of shadows. The opportunity is so fine a thing that it ought oftener to be offered to the light and to yonder handful of long sedges and rushes in a vase. Their slender gray design of shadows upon white walls is better than a tedious, trivial, or anxious device from the shop.

The shadow has all intricacies of perspective simply translated into line and intersecting curve, and pictorially presented to the eyes, not to the mind. The shadow knows nothing except its flat designs, having no third dimension. It is single; it draws a decoration that was never seen before, and will never be seen again, and that, untouched, varies with the journey of the sun, shifts the inter-relation of a score of delicate lines at the mere passing of time, though all the room be motionless. Why will design insist upon its importunate immortality? Wiser is the drama, and wiser the dance, that do not pause upon an attitude. But these walk with passion or pleasure, while the shadow walks with the earth. It alters as the hours wheel.

Moreover, while the habit of your sunward thoughts is still flowing southward, after the winter and the spring, it surprises you in the sudden gleam of a north-westering sun. It decks a new wall; it is shed by a late sunset through a window unvisited for a year past; it betrays the flitting of the sun into unwonted skies—a sun that takes the mid-summer world in the rear, and shows his head at a sally-porte, and is about to alight on an unused horizon. So does the gray drawing, with which you have allowed the sun and your pot of rushes to adorn your room, play the stealthy game of the year.

You need not stint yourself of shadows, for an occasion. It needs but four candles to make a hanging Oriental bell play the most buoyant jugglery overhead. Two lamps make of one palm-branch a symmetrical counterchange of shadows, and here two palm-branches close with one another in shadow, their arches flowing together, and their paler grays darkening. It is hard to believe that there are many to prefer a " repeating pattern."

It must be granted to them that a gray day robs of their decoration the walls that should be sprinkled with shadows. Let, then, a plaque or a picture be kept for hanging on shadowless days. To dress a room once for all, and to give it no more heed, is to neglect the units of the days.

Shadows within doors are yet only messages from that world of shadows which is the landscape of sunshine. Facing a May sun you see little except an infinite number of shadows. Atoms of shadow—be the day bright enough—compose the very air through which you see the light. The trees show you a shadow for every leaf, and the poplars are sprinkled upon the shining sky with little shadows that look translucent. The liveliness of every shadow is that some light is reflected into it; shade and shine have been entangled as though by some wild wind through their million molecules.

By these shadows of mere mid-air the coolness and the dark of night are interlocked with the unclouded sun. Turn sunward from the north, and shadows come to life, and are themselves the life, the action, and the transparence of their day.

To eyes tired and retired all day within lowered blinds, the light looks still and changeless. So many squares of sunshine abide for so many hours, and when the sun has circled away they pass and are extinguished. Him who lies alone there the outer world touches less by this long sunshine than by the haste and passage of a shadow. Although there may be no tree to stand between his window and the south, and although no noonday wind may blow a branch of roses across the blind, shadows and their life will be carried across by a brilliant bird.

To the sick man a cloud-shadow is nothing but an eclipse; he cannot see its shape, its colour, its approach, or its flight. It does but darken his window as it darkens the day, and is gone again; he does not see it pluck and snatch the sun. But the flying bird shows him wings. What flash of light could be more bright for him than such a flash of darkness?

It is the pulse of life, where all change had seemed to be charmed. If he had seen the bird itself he would have seen less—the bird's shadow was a message from the sun.

There are two separated flights for the fancy to
follow, the flight of the bird in the air, and the flight
of its shadow on earth. This goes across the window
blind, across the wood, where it is astray for a while in
the shades; it dips into the valley, growing vaguer and
larger, runs, quicker than the wind, uphill, smaller and
darker on the soft and dry grass, and rushes to meet
its bird when the bird swoops to a branch and
clings.

In the great bird country of the north-eastern littoral
of England, about Holy Island and the basaltic rocks,
the shadows of the high birds are the movement and
the pulse of the solitude. Where there are no woods
to make a shade, the sun suffers the brilliant eclipse
of flocks of pearl-white sea birds, or of the solitary
creature driving on the wind. Theirs is always a surprise of flight. The clouds go one way, but the birds
go all ways: in from the sea or out, across the sands,
inland to high northern fields, where the crops are late
by a month. They fly so high that though they have
the shadow of the sun under their wings, they have
the light of the earth there also. The waves and the
coast shine up to them, and they fly between lights.

Black flocks and white they gather their delicate
shadows up, "swift as dreams," at the end of their
flight into the clefts, platforms, and ledges of harbour-
less rocks dominating the North Sea. They subside
by degrees, with lessening and shortening volleys of
wings and cries until there comes the general shadow
of night wherewith the little shadows close, complete.

The evening is the shadow of another flight. All
the birds have traced wild and innumerable paths across

the mid-May earth; their shadows have fled all day faster than her streams, and have overtaken all the movement of her wingless creatures. But now, at nightfall, it is the flight of the very earth that carries her clasped shadow from the sun.

WOMEN AND BOOKS

THE SEVENTEENTH CENTURY

ALL Englishmen know the name of Lucy Hutchinson; and of her calling and election to the most wifely of all wifehoods—that of a soldier's wife—history has made her countrymen aware. Inasmuch as Colonel Hutchinson was a political soldier, moreover, she is something more than his biographer—his historian. And she convinces her reader that her Puritan principles kept abreast of her affections. There is no self-abandonment; she is not precipitate; keeps her own footing; wife of a soldier as she is, would not have armed him without her own previous indignation against the enemy. She is a soldier at his orders, but she had warily and freely chosen her captain.

Briefly, and with the dignity that the language of her day kept unmarred for her use, she relates her own childhood and youth. She was a child such as those serious times desired that a child should be; that is, she was as slightly a child, and for as brief a time, as might be. Childhood, as an age of progress, was not to be delayed, as an age of imperfection was to be improved, as an age of inability was not to be exposed except when precocity distinguished it. It must at any rate be shortened. Lucy Apsley, at four years old, read English perfectly, and was "carried to sermons, and could remember and repeat them exactly." "At seven she had eight tutors in several qualities." She outstripped her brothers in Latin, albeit they were at school and she had no teacher except her father's chaplain, who, poor gentleman, was "a pitiful dull fellow." She was not companionable. Her many friends were indulged with "babies" (that is, dolls) and these she pulled to pieces. She exhorted the maids, she owned, "much." But she also heard much of their love stories, and acquired a taste for sonnets.

It was a sonnet, and indeed one of her own writing, that brought about her acquaintance with Mr. Hutchinson. The sonnet was read to him, and discussed amongst his friends, with guesses at the authorship; for a young woman did not, in that world, write a sonnet without a feint of hiding its origin. One gentleman believed a woman had made it. Another said, if so, there were but two women capable of making it; but he owned, later, that he said "two" out of civility (very good civility of a kind that is not now practised) to a lady who chanced to be present; but that he knew well there was but one; and he named her. From her future husband Lucy Apsley received that praise of exceptions wherewith women are now, and always will be, praised : "Mr. Hutchinson," she says, "fancying something of rationality in the sonnet beyond the customary reach of a she-wit, could scarcely believe it was a woman's."

He sought her acquaintance, and they were married. Her treasured conscience did not prevent her from noting the jealousy of her young friends. A generous mind, perhaps, would rather itself suffer jealousy than be quick in suspecting, or complacent in causing, or precise in setting it down. But Mrs. Hutchinson doubtless offered up the envy of her companions in homage to her Puritan

lover's splendour. His austerity did not hinder him
from wearing his " fine, thick-set head of hair " in long
locks that were an offence to many of his own sect, but,
she says, " a great ornament to him." But for herself
she has some dissimulated vanities. She was negligent
of dress, and when, after much waiting and many devices, her suitor first saw her, she was " not ugly in a
careless riding-habit." As for him, " in spite of all her
indifference, she was surprised (she writes) with some
unusual liking in her soul when she saw this gentleman,
who had hair, eyes, shape, and countenance enough to
beget love in any one." He married her as soon as she
could leave her chamber, when she was so deformed
by small-pox that " the priest and all that saw her were
affrighted to look at her; but God recompensed his
justice and constancy by restoring her."

The following are some of the admirable sentences
that prove Lucy Hutchinson a woman of letters in a
far more serious sense than our own time uses. One
phrase has a Stevenson-like character, a kind of gesture
of language; this is where she praises her husband's
" handsome management of love." [1] She thus prefaces

[1] It is worth noting that long after the writing of this paper,
and the ascription of a Stevenson-like character to the quoted
phrase, a letter of Stevenson's was published, and proved that
he had read Lucy Hutchinson's writings, and that he did not
love her. "I have possessed myself of Mrs. Hutchinson, whom,
of course, I admire, etc. . . . I sometimes wish the old Colonel had
got drunk and beaten her, in the bitterness of my spirit. . . .
The way in which she talks of herself makes one's blood run
cold." He was young at that time of writing, and perhaps
hardly aware of the lesson in English he had taken from her.
We know that he never wasted the opportunity for such a lesson;

her description of her honoured lord : " If my treacher-
ous memory have not lost the dearest treasure that ever
I committed to its trust——." She boasts of her country
in lofty phrase : " God hath, as it were, enclosed a
people here, out of the waste common of the world."
And again of her husband : " It will be as hard to say
which was the predominant virtue in him as which is
so in its own nature." " He had made up his accounts
with life and death, and fixed his purpose to entertain
both honourably." " The heat of his youth a little inclined him to the passion of anger, and the goodness of
his nature to those of love and grief ; but reason was
never dethroned by them, but continued governor and
moderator of his soul."

She describes sweetly certain three damsels who had
" conceived a kindness " for her lord, their susceptibility,
their willingness, their " admirable tempting beauty,"
and " such excellent good-nature as would have thawed
a rock of ice " ; but she adds no less beautifully, " It
was not his time to love." In her widowhood she remembered that she had been commanded "not to grieve
at the common rate of women " ; and this is the lovely
phrase of her grief : " As his shadow, she waited on him
everywhere, till he was taken to that region of light which
admits of none, and then she vanished into nothing."

She has an invincible anger against the enemies of
her husband and of the cause. The fevers, "little less

and the fact that he did allow her to adminster one to him in
right seventeenth-century diction is established—it is not too
bold to say so—by my recognition of his style in her own. I had
surely caught the retrospective reflex note, heard first in his
voice, recognized in hers.

than plagues," that were common in that age carry
them off exemplarily by families at a time. An adversary
is " the devil's exquisite solicitor." All Royalists are of
" the wicked faction." She suspected his warders of
poisoning Colonel Hutchinson in the prison wherein
he died. The keeper had given him, under pretence
of kindness, a bottle of excellent wine, and the two
gentlemen who drank of it died within four months.
A poison of strange operation! " We must leave it to
the great day when all crimes, how secret soever, will
be made manifest, whether they added poison to all
their other iniquity, whereby they certainly murdered
this guiltless servant of God." When he was near death,
she adds, " a gentlewoman of the Castle came up and
asked him how he did. He told her, Incomparably
well, and full of faith."

On the subject of politics, Mrs. Hutchinson writes,
it must be owned, platitudes; but all are simple, and
some are stated with dignity. Her power, her integrity,
her tenderness, her pomp, the liberal and public interests
of her life, her good breeding, her education, her exquisite diction, are such as may well make a reader ask
how and why the literature of England declined upon
the vulgarity, ignorance, cowardice, foolishness, that
became " feminine " in the estimation of a later age;
that is, in the character of women succeeding her, and
in the estimation of men succeeding her lord. The
noble graces of Lucy Hutchinson, I say, may well
make us marvel at the downfall following—at Gold-
smith's invention of the women of " The Vicar of
Wakefield " in one age, and at Thackeray's invention
of the women of " Esmond " in another.

Mrs. Hutchinson has little leisure for much praise of the natural beauty of sky and landscape, but now and then in her work there appears an abiding sense of the pleasantness of the rural world—in her day an implicit feeling rather than an explicit. " The happiness of the soil and air contribute all things that are necessary to the use or delight of man's life." " He had an opportunity of conversing with her in those pleasant walks which, at the sweet season of the spring, invited all the neighbouring inhabitants to seek their joys." And she describes a dream whereof the scene was in the green fields of Southwark. What an England was hers! And what an English! A memorable vintage of our literature and speech was granted in her day; we owe much to those who—as she did—gathered it in.

MRS. DINGLEY

WE cannot do her honour by her Christian name.[1] All we have to call her by more tenderly is the mere D, the D that ties her to Stella, with whom she made the two-in-one whom Swift loved "better a thousand times than life, as hope saved." MD, without full stops, Swift writes it eight times in a line for the pleasure of writing it. " MD sometimes means Stella alone," says one of many editors. "The letters were written nominally to Stella and Mrs. Dingley," says another, " but it does not require to be said that it was really for Stella's sake alone that they were penned." Not so. "MD " never stands for Stella alone. And the editor does not yet live who shall persuade one honest reader, against the word of Swift, that Swift loved Stella only, with an ordinary love, and not, by a most delicate exception, Stella and Dingley, so joined that they make the "she" and "her" of the letters. And this shall be a paper of reparation to Mrs. Dingley.

No one else in literary history has been so defrauded of her honours. In love "to divide is not to take away," as Shelley says; and Dingley's half of the tender things said to MD is equal to any whole, and takes nothing from the whole of Stella's half. But the sentimentalist has fought against Mrs. Dingley from the outset. He has disliked her, shirked her, misconceived

[1] I found it afterwards; it was Rebecca.

her, and effaced her. Sly sentimentalist—he finds her irksome. Through one of his most modern representatives he has but lately called her a " chaperon." A chaperon!

MD was not a sentimentalist. Stella was not so, though she has been pressed into that character; D certainly was not, and has in this respect been spared by the chronicler; and MD together were " saucy charming MD," " saucy little, pretty, dear rogues," " little monkeys mine," " little mischievous girls," " nautinautinautidear girls," " brats," " huzzies both," " impudence and saucy-face," " saucy noses," " my dearest lives and delights," " dear little young women," " good dallars, not crying dallars " (which means " girls "), " ten thousand times dearest MD," and so forth in a hundred repetitions. They are, every now and then, " poor MD," but obviously not because of their own complaining. Swift called them so because they were mortal; and he, like all great souls, lived and loved, conscious every day of the price, which is death.

The two were joined by love, not without solemnity, though man, with his summary and wholesale readymade sentiment, has thus obstinately put them asunder. No wholesale sentiment can do otherwise than .foolishly play havoc with such a relation. To Swift it was the most secluded thing in the world. " I am weary of friends, and friendships are all monsters, except MD's "; " I ought to read these letters I write after I have done. But I hope it does not puzzle little Dingley to read, for I think I mend: but methinks," he adds, " when I write plain, I do not know how, but we are not alone, all the world can see us. A bad scrawl is so snug; it looks like PMD." Again: "I do not like women so much as I did. MD, you must know, are not women." " God Almighty preserve you both and make us happy together." " I say Amen with all my heart and vitals, that we may never be asunder ten days together while poor Presto lives." " Farewell, dearest beloved MD, and love poor, poor Presto, who has not had one happy day since he left you, as hope saved."

With them—with her—he hid himself in the world, at Court, at the bar of St. James's coffee-house, whither he went on the Irish mail-day, and was " in pain except he saw MD's little handwriting." He hid with them in the long labours of these exquisite letters every night and morning. If no letter came, he comforted himself with thinking that " he had it yet to be happy with." And the world has agreed to hide under its own manifold and lachrymose blunders the grace and singularity—the distinction—of this sweet romance. " Little, sequestered pleasure-house "— it seemed as though " the many could not miss it," but not even the few have found it.

It is part of the scheme of the sympathetic historian that Stella should be the victim of hope deferred, watching for letters from Swift. But day and night Presto complains of the scantiness of MD's little letters; he waits upon " her " will: " I shall make a sort of journal, and when it is full I will send it whether MD writes or not; and so that will be pretty." " Naughty girls that will not write to a body ! " " I wish you were whipped for forgetting to send. Go, be far enough, negligent baggages." " You, Mistress Stella, shall write your share, and then comes Dingley altogether, and then Stella a little crumb at the end; and then conclude with something handsome and genteel, as 'your most humble cumdumble.'" But Scott and Macaulay and Thackeray are all exceedingly sorry for a pining Stella. Thackeray represents her wearing out her life in wait for Swift's "cold heart."

Swift is most charming when he is feigning to complain of his task: "Here is such a stir and bustle with this little MD of ours; I must be writing every night; O Lord, O Lord!" "I must go write idle things, and twittle twattle." "These saucy jades take up so much of my time with writing to them in the morning." Is it not a stealthy wrong done upon Mrs. Dingley that she should be stripped of all these ornaments to her name and memory? When Swift tells a woman in a letter that there he is "writing in bed, like a tiger," she should go gay in the eyes of all generations.

They will not let Stella go gay, because of sentiment; and they will not let Mrs. Dingley go gay, because of sentiment for Stella. Marry come up! Why did not the historians assign all the tender passages (taken very tearfully) to Stella, and let Dingley have the jokes, then? That would have been no ill share for Dingley. But no, forsooth, Dingley is allowed nothing.

There are passages, nevertheless, which can hardly be taken from her. For now and then Swift parts his dear MD. When he does so he invariably drops those initials and writes "Stella" or "Ppt" for the one, and "D" or "Dingley" for the other. There is no exception to this anywhere. He is anxious about Stella's "little eyes," and about her health generally; whereas Dingley is strong. Poor Ppt, he thinks, will not catch

the "new fever," because she is not well; "but why
should D escape it, pray?" And Mrs. Dingley is rebuked for her tale of a journey from Dublin to Wex-
ford. "I doubt, Madam Dingley, you are apt to lie in
your travels, though not so bad as Stella; she tells
thumpers." Stella is often reproved for her spelling, and
Mrs. Dingley writes much the better hand. But she is
a puzzle-headed woman, like another. "What do you
mean by my fourth letter, Madam Dinglibus? Does
not Stella say you had my fifth, goody Blunder?"
"Now, Mistress Dingley, are you not an impudent
slut to expect a letter next packet? Unreasonable baggage! No, little Dingley, I am always in bed by twelve,
and I take great care of myself." "You are a pretending slut, indeed, with your 'fourth' and 'fifth' in the
margin, and your 'journal' and everything. O Lord,
never saw the like, we shall never have done." "I
never saw such a letter, so saucy, so journalish, so
everything." Swift is insistently grateful for their in-
quiries for his health. He pauses seriously to thank
them in the midst of his prattle. Both women—MD—
are rallied on their politics: "I have a fancy that Ppt
is a Tory, I fancy she looks like one, and D a sort of
trimmer."

But it is for Dingley separately that Swift endured a
wild bird in his lodgings. His man Patrick had got one
to take over to her in Ireland. "He keeps it in a closet,
where it makes a terrible litter; but I say nothing; I
am as tame as a clout."

Forgotten Dingley, happy in this, has not had to
endure the ignominy, in a hundred modern essays, to
be retrospectively offered to Swift as an unclaimed wife;

so far so good. But two hundred years is long for her to have gone stripped of so radiant a glory as is hers by right. "Better, thanks to MD's prayers," wrote the immortal man who loved her, in a private fragment of a journal, never meant for Dingley's eyes, nor for Ppt's, nor for any human eyes; and the rogue Stella has for two centuries been made to steal all the credit of those prayers, and all the thanks of that pious benediction.

PRUE

THROUGH the long history of human relations, which is the history of the life of our race, there sounds at intervals the clamour of a single voice which has not the tone of oratory, but asks, answers, interrupts itself, interrupts—what else? Whatever else it interrupts is silence; there are pauses, but no answers. There is the jest without the laugh, and again the laugh without the jest. And this is because the letters written by Madame de Sévigné were all saved, and not many written to her; because Swift burnt the letters that were the dearest things in life to him, while "MD" both made a treasury of his; and because Prue kept all the letters which Steele wrote to her from their marriage-day onwards, and Steele kept none of hers.

In Swift's case the silence is full of echoes; that is to say, his letters repeat the phrases of Stella's and Dingley's, to play with them, flout them, and toss them back against the two silenced voices. He never lets the word of these two women fall to the ground; and when they have but blundered with it, and aimed it wide, and sent it weakly, he will catch it, and play you twenty delicate and expert juggling pranks with it as he sends it back into their innocent faces. So we have something of MD's letters in the "Journal," and this in the only form in which we desire them, to tell the truth; for when Swift gravely saves us some specimens of Stella's wit, after her death, as she spoke them, and not as he mimicked them, they make a sorry show.

In many correspondences, where one voice remains and the other is gone, the retort is enough for two. It is as when, the other day, the half of a pretty quarrel between nurse and child came down from an upper floor to the ears of a mother who decided that she need not interfere. The voice of the undaunted child it was that was audible alone, and it replied, " I'm not; *you* are "; and anon, " I'll tell *yours.*" Nothing was really missing there.

But Steele's letters to Prue, his wife, are no such simple matter. The turn we shall give them depends upon the unheard tone whereto they reply. And there is room for conjecture. It has pleased the more modern of the many spirits of banter to supply Prue's eternal silence with the voice of a scold. It is painful to me to complain of Thackeray; but see what a figure he makes of Prue in " Esmond." It is, says the nineteenth-century humourist, in defence against the pursuit of a jealous, exacting, neglected, or evaded wife that poor Dick Steele sends those little notes of excuse: " Dearest Being on earth, pardon me if you do not see me till eleven o'clock, having met a schoolfellow from India "; " My dear, dear wife, I write to let you know I do not come home to dinner, being obliged to attend some business abroad, of which I shall give you an account (when I see you in the evening), as becomes your dutiful and obedient husband "; " Dear Prue, I cannot come home to dinner. I languish for your welfare "; " I stay here in order to get Tonson to

discount a bill for me, and shall dine with him to
that end"; and so forth. Once only does Steele really
afford the recent humourist the suggestion that is apparently always so welcome. It is when he writes that he
is invited to supper to Mr. Boyle's, and adds: "Dear
Prue, do not send after me, for I shall be ridiculous."
But even this is to be read not ungracefully by a well-
graced reader. Prue was young and unused to the
world. Her husband, by the way, had been already
married; and his greater age makes his constant
deference all the more charming.

But with this one exception, Steele's little notes,
kept by his wife while she lived, and treasured after her
death by her daughter and his, are no record of the
watchings and dodgings of a London farce. It is worth
while to remember that Steele's dinner, which it was
so often difficult to eat at home, was a thing of midday,
and therefore of mid-business. But that is a detail.
What is desirable is that a reasonable degree of sweetness should be attributed to Prue; for it is no more
than just. To her Steele wrote in a dedication: "How
often has your tenderness removed pain from my ach-
ing head, how often anguish from my afflicted heart.
If there are such beings as guardian angels, they are
thus employed. I cannot believe one of them to be
more good in inclination, or more charming in form,
than my wife."

True, this was for the public; but not so were these
daily notes; and these carry to her his assurance that
she is "the beautifullest object in the world. I know
no happiness in this life in any degree comparable to
the pleasure I have in your person and society." "But

indeed, though you have every perfection, you have an extravagant fault, which almost frustrates the good in you to me; and that is, that you do not love to dress, to appear, to shine out, even at my request, and to make me proud of you, or rather to indulge the pride I have that you are mine." The correction of the phrase is finely considerate.

Prue cannot have been a dull wife, for this last compliment is a reply, full of polite alacrity, to a letter from her asking for a little flattery. How assiduously, and with what a civilized absence of uncouthness, of shame-facedness, and of slang of the mind, with what simplicity, alertness, and finish, does he step out at her invitation, and perform! She wanted a compliment, though they had been long married then, and he immediately turned it. This was no dowdy Prue.

Her request, by the way, which he repeats in obeying it, is one of the few instances of the other side of the correspondence—one of the few direct echoes of that one of the two voices which is silent.

The ceremony of the letters and the deferent method of address and signature are never dropped in this most intimate of letter-writing. It is not a little depressing to think that in this very form and state is supposed, by the modern reader, to lurk the stealthiness of the husband of farce, the "rogue." One does not like the word. Is it not clownish to apply it with intention to the husband of Prue? He did not pay, he was always in difficulties, he hid from bailiffs, he did many other things that tarnish honour, more or less, and things for which he had to beg Prue's special pardon; but yet he is not a fit subject for the unhandsome incredulity which is proud to be always at hand with an ironic commentary on such letters as his.

I have no wish to bowdlerize Sir Richard Steele, his ways and words. He wrote to Prue at night when the burgundy had been too much for him, and in the morning after. He announces that he is coming to her "within a pint of wine." One of his gayest letters—a love-letter before the marriage, addressed to "dear lovely Mrs. Scurlock"—confesses candidly that he had been pledging her too well: "I have been in very good company, where your health, under the chara&cter of the woman I loved best, has been often drunk; so that I may say that I am dead drunk for your sake, which is more than *I die for you*."

Steele obviously drank burgundy wildly, as did his "good company"; as did also the admirable Addison, who was so solitary in chara&cter and so serene in temperament. But no one has, for this fault, the right to put a railing accusation into the mouth of Prue. Every woman has a right to her own silence, whether her silence be hers of set purpose or by accident. And every creature has a right to security from the banterings peculiar to the humourists of a succeeding age. To every century its own ironies, to every century its own vulgarities. In Steele's time they had theirs. They might have rallied Prue more coarsely, but it would have been with a different rallying. Writers of the nineteenth century went about to rob her of her grace.

She kept some four hundred of these little letters of her lord's. It was a loyal keeping. But what does Thackeray call it? His word is "thrifty." He says: "There are four hundred letters of Dick Steele's to his wife, which that thrifty woman preserved accurately."

"Thrifty" is a hard word to apply to her whom Steele styled, in the year before her death, his "charming little insolent." She was ill in Wales, and he, at home, wept upon her pillow, and "took it to be a sin to go to sleep." Thrifty they may call her, and accurate if they will; but she lies in Westminster Abbey, and Steele called her "your Prueship."

MRS. JOHNSON

THIS paper shall not be headed "Tetty." What
may be a graceful enough freedom with the
wives of other men shall be prohibited in the case of
Johnson's, she with whose name no writer until now
has scrupled to take freedoms whereto all graces were
lacking. "Tetty" it should not be, if for no other
reason, for this—that the chance of writing "Tetty"
as a title is a kind of facile literary opportunity; it
shall be denied. The Essay owes thus much amends
of deliberate care to Dr. Johnson's wife. But, indeed,
the reason is graver. What wish would he have had
but that the language in the making whereof he took
no ignoble part should somewhere, at some time, treat
his only friend with ordinary honour?

Men who would trust Dr. Johnson with their
orthodoxy, with their vocabulary, and with the most
intimate vanity of their human wishes, refuse, with
every mark of insolence, to trust him in regard to his
wife. On that one point no reverence is paid to him,
no deference, no respect, not so much as the credit
due to our common sanity. Yet he is not reviled on
account of his Thrale—nor, indeed, is his Thrale now
seriously reproached for her Piozzi. It is true that
Macaulay, preparing himself and his reader "in his
well-known way" (as a rustic of Mr. Hardy's might
have it) for the recital of her second marriage, says

that it would have been well if she had been laid beside the kind and generous Thrale when, in the prime of her life, he died. But Macaulay has not left us heirs to his indignation. His well-known way was to exhaust those possibilities of effect in which the commonplace is so rich. And he was permitted to point his paragraphs as he would, not only by calling Mrs. Thrale's attachment to her second husband "a degrading passion," but by summoning a chorus of "all London" to the same purpose. She fled, he tells us, from the laughter and hisses of her countrymen and countrywomen to a land where she was unknown. Thus when Macaulay chastises Mrs. Elizabeth Porter for marrying Johnson, he is not inconsistent, for he pursues Mrs. Thrale with equal rigour for her audacity in keeping gaiety and grace in her mind and manners longer than Macaulay liked to see such ornaments added to the charm of twice "married brows."

It is not so with succeeding essayists. One of these minor biographers is so gentle as to call the attachment of Mrs. Thrale and Piozzi "a mutual affection." He adds, "No one who has had some experience of life will be inclined to condemn Mrs. Thrale." But there is no such courtesy, even from him, for Mrs. Johnson. Neither to him nor to any other writer has it yet occurred that if England loves her great Englishman's memory, she owes not only courtesy, but gratitude, to the only woman who loved him while there was yet time.

Not a thought of that debt has stayed the alacrity with which a caricature has been acclaimed as the only possible portrait of Mrs. Johnson. Garrick's school reminiscences would probably have made a much more charming woman grotesque. Garrick is welcome to his remembrances; we may even reserve for ourselves the liberty of envying those who heard him. But honest laughter should not fall into that tone of common antithesis which seems to say, "See what are the absurdities of the great! Such is life! On this one point we, even we, are wiser than Dr. Johnson—we know how grotesque was his wife. We know something of the privacies of her toilet-table. We are able to compare her figure with the figures we, unlike him in his youth, have had the opportunity of admiring—the figures of the well-bred and well-dressed." It is a sorry success to be able to say so much.

But in fact such a triumph belongs to no man. When Samuel Johnson, at twenty-six, married his wife, he gave the dull an advantage over himself which none but the dullest will take. He chose, for love, a woman who had the wit to admire him at first meeting, and in spite of first sight. "That," she said to her daughter, "is the most sensible man I ever met." He was penniless. She had what was no mean portion for those times and those conditions; and, granted that she was affected, and provincial, and short, and all the rest with which she is charged, she was probably not without suitors; nor do her defects or faults seem to have been those of an unadmired or neglected woman. Next, let us remember what was the aspect of Johnson's form and face, even in his twenties, and how little he could have touched the senses of a widow fond of externals. This one loved him, accepted him, made him happy, gave to one of the noblest of all

English hearts the one love of its sombre life. And English literature has had no better phrase for her than Macaulay's—" She accepted, with a readiness which did her little honour, the addresses of a suitor who might have been her son."

Her readiness did her incalculable honour. But it is at last worth remembering that Johnson had first done her incalculable honour. No one has given to man or woman the right to judge as to the worthiness of her who received it. The meanest man is generally allowed his own counsel as to his own wife; one of the greatest of men has been denied it. "The lover," says Macaulay, "continued to be under the illusions of the wedding day till the lady died." What is so graciously said is not enough. He was under those "illusions" until he too died, when he had long passed her latest age, and was therefore able to set right that balance of years which has so much irritated the impertinent. Johnson passed from this life twelve years older than she, and so for twelve years his constant eyes had to turn backwards to dwell upon her. Time gave him a younger wife.

And here I will put into Mrs. Johnson's mouth, that mouth to which no one else has ever attributed any beautiful sayings, the words of Marceline Desbordes-Valmore to the young husband she loved: "Older than thou! Let me never see thou knowest it. Forget it! I will remember it, to die before thy death."

Macaulay, in his unerring effectiveness, uses Johnson's short sight for an added affront to Mrs. Johnson. The bridegroom was too weak of eyesight "to distinguish ceruse from natural bloom." Nevertheless, he saw well enough, when he was old, to distinguish Mrs. Thrale's dresses. He reproved her for wearing a dark dress; it was unsuitable, he said, for her size; a little creature should show gay colours "like an insect." We are not called upon to admire his wife; why, then, our taste being thus uncompromised, do we not suffer him to admire her? It is the most gratuitous kind of intrusion. Moreover, the biographers are eager to permit that touch of romance and grace in his relations to Mrs. Thrale, which they officially deny in the case of Mrs. Johnson. But the difference is all on the other side. He would not have bidden his wife dress like an insect. Mrs. Thrale was to him "the first of womankind" only because his wife was dead.

Beauclerc, we learn, was wont to cap Garrick's mimicry of Johnson's love-making by repeating the words of Johnson himself in after-years—"It was a love-match on both sides." And obviously he was as strange a lover as they said. Who doubted it? Was there any other woman in England to give such a suitor the opportunity of an eternal love? "A life radically wretched," was the life of this master of Letters; but she, who has received nothing in return except ignominy from these unthankful Letters, had been alone to make it otherwise. Well for him that he married so young as to earn the ridicule of all the biographers in England; for by doing so he, most happily, possessed his wife for nearly twenty years. I have called her his only friend. So indeed she was, though he had followers, disciples, rivals, competitors, and companions, many degrees of admirers, a biographer, a patron, and a public. He had also the houseful of sad old women who quarrelled under his beneficent protection. But what friend had he? He was "solitary" from the day she died.

Let us consider under what solemn conditions and in what immortal phrase the word "solitary" stands. He wrote it, all Englishmen know where. He wrote it in the hour of that melancholy triumph when he had been at last set free from the dependence upon hope. He hoped no more, and he needed not to hope. The "notice" of Lord Chesterfield had been too long deferred; it was granted at last, when it was a flattery which Johnson's court of friends would applaud. But not for their sake was it welcome. To no living ear would he bring it and report it with delight.

He was indifferent, he was known. The sensitiveness to pleasure was gone, and the sensitiveness to pain, slights, and neglect would thenceforth be suffered to rest; no man in England would put that to proof again. No man in England, did I say? But, indeed, that is not so. No slight to him, to his person, or to his fame could have had power to cause him pain more sensibly than the customary, habitual, ready-made ridicule that has been cast by posterity upon her whom he loved for twenty years, prayed for during thirty-two years more, who satisfied one of the saddest human hearts, but to whom the world, assiduous to admire him, hardly accords human dignity. He wrote praises of her manners and of her person for her tomb. But her epitaph, that does not name her, is in the greatest of English prose. What was favour to him? "I am indifferent. . . . I am known. . . . I am solitary, and cannot impart it."

MADAME ROLAND

THE articulate heroine has her reward of appreciation and her dues of praise; it is her appropriate fortune to have it definitely measured, and generally on equal terms. She takes pains to explain herself, and is understood, and pitied, when need is, on the right occasions. For instance, Madame Roland, a woman of merit, who knew her "merit's name and place," addressed her memoirs, her studies in contemporary history, her autobiography, her many speeches, and her last phrase at the foot of the undaunting scaffold, to a great audience of her equals (more or less) then living and to live in the ages then to come—her equals and those she raises to her own level, as the heroic example has authority to do.

Another woman—the Queen—suffered at that time, and suffered without the command of language, the exactitude of phrase, the precision of judgement, the proffer of prophecy, the explicit sense of Innocence and Moderation oppressed in her person. These were Madame Roland's; but the other woman, without eloquence, without literature, and without any judicial sense of history, addresses no mere congregation of readers. Marie Antoinette's unrecorded pangs pass into the treasuries of the experience of the whole human family. All that are human have some part there; genius itself may lean in contemplation over that abyss

of woe; the great poets themselves may look into its
distances and solitudes. Compassion here has no measure
and no language. Madame Roland speaks neither to
genius nor to complete simplicity; Marie Antoinette
holds her peace in the presence of each, dumb in her
presence.

Madame Roland had no dumbness of the spirit, as
history, prompted by her own musical voice, presents
her to a world well prepared to do her justice. Of
that justice she had full expectation; justice here,
justice in the world—the world that even when universal philosophy should reign would be inevitably the
world of mediocrity; justice that would come of en-
lightened views; justice that would be the lesson learnt
by the nations widely educated up to some point generally accessible; justice well within earthly sight and
competence. This confidence was also her reward.
For what justice did the Queen look? Here it is the
" abyss that appeals to the abyss."

Twice only in the life of Madame Roland is there
a lapse into silence, and for the record of these two
poor failures of that long, indomitable, reasonable, tem-
perate, explicit utterance which expressed her life and
mind we are debtors to her friends. She herself has
not confessed them. Nowhere else, whether in her
candid history of herself, or in her wise history of her
country, or in her judicial history of her contemporaries, whose spirit she discerned, whose powers she
appraised, whose errors she foresaw; hardly in her
thought, and never in her word, is a break to be perceived; she is not silent and she hardly stammers; and
when she tells us of her tears—the tears of youth only

—her record is voluble and all complete. For the dignity of her style, of her force, and of her balanced character, Madame Roland would doubtless have effaced the two imperfections which, to us who would be glad to admire in silence her heroic figure, if that heroic figure would but cease to talk, are finer and more noble than her well-placed language and the high successes of her decision and her endurance. More than this, the two failures of this unfailing woman are two little doors opened suddenly into those wider spaces and into that dominion of solitude which, after all, do doubtless exist even in the most garrulous soul. By these two outlets Manon Roland also reaches the region of Marie Antoinette. But they befell her at the close of her life, and they shall be named at the end of this brief study.

Madame Roland may seem the more heroic to those whose suffrages she seeks in all times and nations because of the fact that she manifestly suppresses in her self-descriptions any signs of a natural gaiety. Her memoirs give evidence of no such thing; it is only in her letters, not intended for the world, that we are aware of the inadvertence of moments. We may overhear a laugh at times, but not in those consciously sprightly hours that she spent with her convent-school friend gathering fruit and counting eggs at the farm. She pursued these country tasks not without offering herself the cultivated congratulation of one whom cities had failed to allure, and who bore in mind the examples of Antiquity. She did not forget the death of Socrates. Or, rather, she finds an occasion to reproach herself with having once forgotten it, and with having omitted

what another might have considered the tedious recollection of the condemnation of Phocion. She never
wearied of these examples. But it is her inexhaustible
freshness in these things that has helped other writers
of her time to weary us.

In her manner of telling her story there is an absence of all exaggeration, which gives the reader a
constant sense of security. That virtue of style and
thought was one she proposed to herself and attained
with exact consciousness of success. It would be almost
enough (in the perfection of her practice) to make a
great writer; even a measure of it goes far to make a
fair one. Her moderation of statement is never shaken;
and if she now and then glances aside from her direct
narrative road to hazard a conjecture, the error she
may make is on the generous side of hope and faith.
For instance, she is too sure that her Friends (so she
always calls the *Girondins*, using no nicknames) are
safe, whereas they were then all doomed; a young
man who had carried a harmless message for her—a
mere notification to her family of her arrest—receives
her cheerful commendation for his good feeling; from
a note we learn that for this action he suffered on the
scaffold and that his father soon thereafter died of grief.
But Madame Roland never matched such a delirious
event as this by any delirium of her own imagination.
The delirium was in things and in the acts of men;
her mind was never hurried from its sane self-pos-
session, when the facts raved.

It was only when she used the rhetoric ready to her
hand that she stooped to verbal violence; *et encore!*
References to the banishment of Aristides and the

hemlock of Socrates had become toy daggers and bend-
ing swords in the hands of her compatriots, and she is
hardly to be accused of violence in brandishing those
weapons. Sometimes, refuse rhetoric being all too
ready, she takes it on her pen, in honest haste, as
though it were honest speech, and stands committed
to such a phrase as this: "The dregs of the nation
placed such a one at the helm of affairs."

But her manner was not generally to write anything but a clear and efficient French language. She
never wrote for the love of art, but without some
measure of art she did not write; and her simplicity
is somewhat altered by that importunate love of the
Antique. In " Bleak House " there is an old lady who
insisted that the name " Mr. Turveydrop," as it appeared polished on the door-plate of the dancing
master, was the name of the pretentious father and
not of the industrious son—albeit, needless to say, one
name was common to them. With equal severity I
aver that when Madame Roland wrote to her husband
in the second person singular she was using the *tu* of
Rome and not the *tu* of Paris. French was indeed the
language; but had it been French in spirit she would
(in spite of the growing Republican fashion) have said
vous to this " homme éclairé, de mœurs pures, à qui
l'on ne peut reprocher que sa grande admiration pour
les anciens aux dépens des modernes qu'il méprise, et
le faible de trop aimer à parler de lui." There was no
French *tu* in her relations with this husband, gravely
esteemed and appraised, discreetly rebuked, the best
passages of whose Ministerial reports she wrote, and
whom she observed as he slowly began to think he

himself had composed them. She loved him with a loyal, obedient, and discriminating affection, and when she had been put to death, he, still at liberty, fell upon his sword.

This last letter was written at a moment when, in order to prevent the exposure of a public death, Madame Roland had intended to take opium in the end of her cruel imprisonment. A little later she chose that those who oppressed her country should have their way with her to the last. But, while still intending self-destruction, she had written to her husband: "Forgive me, respectable man, for disposing of a life that I had consecrated to thee." In quoting this I mean to make no too-easy effect with the word "respectable," grown grotesque by the tedious gibe of our own present fashion of speech.

Madame Roland, I have said, was twice inarticulate; she had two spaces of silence; one when she, pure and selfless patriot, had heard her condemnation to death. Passing out of the court she beckoned to her friends, and signified to them her sentence "by a gesture." And again there was a pause, in the course of her last days, during which her speeches had not been few, and had been spoken with her beautiful voice unmarred; "she leant," says Riouffe, "alone against her window, and wept there three hours."

THE DARLING YOUNG

FELLOW TRAVELLERS WITH A
BIRD

TO attend to a living child is to be baffled in your
humour, disappointed of your pathos, and set
freshly free from all the pre-occupations. You cannot
anticipate him. Blackbirds, overheard year by year, do
not compose the same phrases; never two leitmotifs
alike. Not the tone, but the note alters. So with the
uncovenanted ways of a child you keep no tryst. They
meet you at another place, after failing you where you
tarried; your former experiences, your documents are
at fault. You are the fellow traveller of a bird. The
bird alights and escapes out of time to your footing.

No man's fancy could be beforehand, for instance,
with a girl of four years old who dictated a letter to a
distant cousin, with the sweet and unimaginable message: "I hope you enjoy yourself with your loving
dolls." A boy, still younger, persuading his mother to
come down from the heights and play with him on the
floor, but sensible, perhaps, that there was a dignity to
be observed none the less, entreated her, " Mother, do
be a lady frog." None ever said their good things
before these indeliberate authors. Even their own kind
—children—have not preceded them. No child in the
past ever found the same replies as the girl of five
whose father made that appeal to feeling which is

doomed to a different, perverse, and unforeseen success. He was rather tired with writing, and had a mind to snare some of the yet uncaptured flock of her sympathies. "Do you know, I have been working hard, darling? I work to buy things for you." "Do you work," she asked, "to buy the lovely puddin's?" Yes, even for these. The subject must have seemed to her to be worth pursuing. "And do you work to buy the fat? I don't like fat."

The sympathies, nevertheless, are there. The same child was to be soothed at night after a weeping dream that a skater had been drowned in the Kensington Round Pond. It was suggested to her that she should forget it by thinking about the one unfailing and gay subject—her wishes. "Do you know," she said, without loss of time, "what I should like best in all the world? A thundred dolls and a whistle!" Her mother was so overcome by this tremendous numeral, that she could make no offer as to the dolls. But the whistle seemed practicable. "It is for me to whistle for cabs," said the child, with a sudden moderation, "when I go to parties." Another morning she came down radiant. "Did you hear a great noise in the miggle of the night? That was me crying. I cried because I dreamt that Cuckoo [a brother] had swallowed a bead into his nose."

The mere errors of children are unforeseen as nothing is—no, nothing feminine—in this adult world. "I've got a lotter than you," is the word of a very young egotist. An older child says, "I'd better go, bettern't I, mother?" He calls a little space at the back of a London house, "the backy-garden." A little creature

proffers almost daily the reminder at luncheon—at
tart-time: "Father, I hope you will remember that I
am the favourite of the crust." Moreover, if an author
set himself to invent the naïf things that children
might do in their Christmas plays at home, he would
hardly light upon the device of the little *troupe* who,
having no footlights, arranged upon the floor a long
row of candle-shades.

"It's *jolly* dull without you, mother," says a little
girl who—gentlest of the gentle—has a dramatic sense
of slang, of which she makes no secret. But she drops
her voice somewhat to disguise her feats of metathesis,
about which she has doubts and which are involuntary:
the "stand-wash," the "sweeping-crosser," the "sewing chamine." Genoese peasants have the same prank
when they try to speak Italian.

Children forget last year so well that if they are
Londoners they should by any means have an impression of the country or the sea annually. A London
little girl watches a fly upon the wing, follows it with
her pointing finger, and names it "bird." Her brother,
who wants to play with a bronze Japanese lobster, asks
"Will you please let me have that tiger?"

At times children give to a word that slight variety
which is the most touching kind of newness. Thus, a
child of three asks you to save him. How moving a
word, and how freshly said! He had heard of the
"saving" of other things of interest—especially chocolate creams taken for safe-keeping—and he asks, "Who
is going to save me to-day? Nurse is going out, will
you save me, mother?" The same little variant upon
common use is in another child's courteous reply to a

summons to help in the arrangement of some flowers,
" I am quite at your ease."

A child, unconscious little author of things told in
this record, was taken lately to see a fellow author of
somewhat different standing from her own, inasmuch
as he is, among other things, a Saturday Reviewer.
As he dwelt in a part of the South-west of the town
unknown to her, she noted with interest the shops of
the neighbourhood as she went, for they might be
those of the *fournisseurs* of her friend. " That is his
bread shop, and that is his book shop. And that,
mother," she said finally, with even heightened sympathy, pausing before a blooming *parterre* of con-
fectionery hard by the abode of her man of letters,
" that, I suppose, is where he buys his sugar pigs."

In all her excursions into streets new to her, this
same child is intent upon a certain quest—the quest of
a genuine collector. We have all heard of collecting
butterflies, of collecting china-dogs, of collecting cocked
hats, and so forth; but her pursuit gives her a joy that
costs her nothing except a sharp look-out upon the
proper names over all shop-windows. No hoard was
ever lighter than hers. " I began three weeks ago next
Monday, mother," she says with precision, " and I have
got thirty-nine." " Thirty-nine what ?" " Smiths."

The mere gathering of children's language would be
much like collecting together a handful of flowers that
should be all unique, single of their kind. In one
thing, however, do children agree, and that is the re-
jection of most of the conventions of the authors who
have reported them. They do not, for example, say
" me is "; their natural reply to " are you ?" is " I are."

One child, pronouncing sweetly and neatly, will have nothing but the nominative pronoun. "Lift I up and let I see it raining," she bids; and told that it does not rain, resumes, "Lift I up and let I see it not raining."

An elder child had a rooted dislike to a brown corduroy suit ordered for her by maternal authority. She wore the garments under protest, and with some resentment. At the same time it was evident that she took no pleasure in hearing her praises sweetly sung by a poet, her friend. He had imagined the making of this child in the counsels of Heaven, and the decreeing of her soft skin, of her brilliant eyes, and of her hair— "a brown tress." She had gravely heard the words as "a brown dress," and she silently bore the poet a grudge for having been the accessory of Providence in the mandate that she should wear the loathed corduroy. The unpractised ear played another little girl a like turn. She had a phrase for snubbing any anecdote that sounded improbable. "That," she said, more or less after Sterne, "is a cotton-wool story."

The learning of words is, needless to say, continued long after the years of mere learning to speak. The young child now takes a current word into use, a little at random, and now makes a new one, so as to save the interruption of a pause for search. I have certainly detected, in children old enough to show their motives, a conviction that a word of their own making is as good a communication as another, and as intelligible. There is even a general implicit conviction among them that the grown-up people, too, make words by the wayside as occasion befalls. How otherwise should words be so numerous that every day brings forward some hitherto unheard? The child would be surprised to know how irritably poets are refused the faculty and authority which he thinks to belong to the common world.

There is something very cheerful and courageous in the setting-out of a child on a journey of speech with so small baggage and with so much confidence in the chances of the hedge. He goes free, a simple adventurer. Nor does he make any officious effort to invent anything strange or particularly expressive or descriptive. The child trusts genially to his hearer. A very young boy, excited by his first sight of sunflowers, was eager to describe them, and called them, without allowing himself to be checked for the trifle of a name, "summersets." This was simple and unexpected; so was the comment of a sister a very little older. "Why does he call those flowers summersets?" their mother said; and the girl, with a darkly brilliant look of humour and penetration, answered, "because they are so big." There seemed to be no further question possible after an explanation that was presented thus charged with meaning.

To a later phase of life, when a little girl's vocabulary was, somewhat at random, growing larger, belong a few brave phrases hazarded to express a meaning well realized—a personal matter. Questioned as to the eating of an uncertain number of buns just before lunch, the child averred, "I took them just to appetize my hunger." As she betrayed a familiar knowledge of the tariff of an attractive confectioner, she was asked whether she and her sisters had been frequenting those little tables on their way from school. " I sometimes go in there, mother," she confessed; " but I generally speculate outside."

Children sometimes attempt to cap something perfectly funny with something so flat that you are obliged to turn the conversation. Dryden does the same thing, not with jokes, but with his sublimer passages. But sometimes a child's deliberate banter is quite intelligible to elders. Take the letter written by a little girl to a mother who had, it seems, allowed her family to see that she was inclined to be satisfied with something of her own writing. The child has a full and gay sense of the sweetest kinds of irony. There was no need for her to write, she and her mother being both at home, but the words must have seemed to her worthy of a pen :— " My dear mother, I really wonder how you can be proud of that article, if it is worthy to be called a article, which I doubt. Such a unletterary article. I cannot call it letterature. I hope you will not write any more such unconventionan trash."

This is the saying of a little boy who admired his much younger sister, and thought her forward for her age : " I wish people knew just how old she is, mother, then they would know she is onward. They can see she is pretty, but they can't know she is such a onward baby."

Thus speak the naturally unreluctant; but there are other children who in time betray a little consciousness and a slight *méfiance* as to where the adult sense of humour may be lurking in wait for them, obscure. These children may not be shy enough to suffer any self-checking in their talk, but they are now and then to be heard slurring a word of which they do not feel

too sure. A little girl whose sensitiveness was barely
enough to cause her to stop to choose between two
words, was wont to bring a cup of tea to the writing-
table of her mother, who had often feigned indignation at the weakness of what her Irish maid always
called " the infusion." " I'm afraid it's bosh again,
mother," said the child; and then, in a half-whisper,
" Is bosh right, or wash, mother?" She was not told,
and decided for herself, with doubts, for bosh. The
afternoon cup left the kitchen an infusion, and reached
the library " bosh " thenceforward.

THE CHILD OF TUMULT

A POPPY bud, packed into tight bundles by so hard and resolute a hand that the petals of the flower never afterwards lose the creases, is a type of the child. Nothing but the unfolding, which is as yet in the non-existing future, can explain the manner of the close folding of character. In both flower and child it looks much as though the process had been the reverse of what it was—as though a finished and open thing had been folded up into the bud—so plainly and certainly is the future implied, and the intention of compressing and folding-close made manifest.

With the other incidents of childish character, the crowd of impulses called "naughtiness" is perfectly perceptible—it would seem heartless to say how soon. The naughty child (who is often an angel of tenderness and charm, affectionate beyond the capacity of his fellows, and a very ascetic of penitence when the time comes) opens early his brief campaigns and raises the standard of revolt as soon as he is capable of the desperate joys of disobedience.

But even the naughty child is an individual, and must not be treated in the mass. He is numerous indeed, but not general, and to describe him you must take the unit, with all his incidents and his organic qualities as they are. Take then, for instance, one naughty child in the reality of his life. He is but six

235

years old, slender and masculine, and not wronged by
long hair, curls, or effeminate dress. His face is delicate
and too often haggard with tears of penitence that
Justice herself would be glad to spare him. Some
beauty he has, and his mouth especially is so lovely as
to seem not only angelic but itself an angel. He has
absolutely no self-control and his passions find him
without defence. They come upon him in the midst
of his usual brilliant gaiety and cut short the frolic
comedy of his fine spirits.

Then for a wild hour he is the enemy of the laws.
If you imprison him, you may hear his resounding
voice as he takes a running kick at the door, shouting
his justification in unconquerable rage. "I'm good
now!" is made as emphatic as a shot by the blow of
his heel upon the panel. But if the moment of forgive-
ness is deferred, in the hope of a more promising repentance, it is only too likely that he will betake himself to a hostile silence and use all the revenge yet
known to his imagination. "Darling mother, open the
door!" cries his touching voice at last; but if the
answer should be "I must leave you for a short time,
for punishment," the storm suddenly thunders again.
"There (crash!) I have broken a plate, and I'm glad it
is broken into such little pieces that you can't mend it.
I'm going to break the 'leftric light." When things
are at this pass there is one way, and only one, to
bring the child to an overwhelming change of mind;
but it is a way that would be cruel, used more than
twice or thrice in his whole career of tempest and defiance. This is to let him see that his mother is
troubled. "Oh, don't cry! Oh, don't be sad!" he

roars, unable still to deal with his own passionate anger, which is still dealing with him. With his kicks of rage he suddenly mingles a dance of apprehension lest his mother should have tears in her eyes. Even while he is still explicitly impenitent and defiant he tries to pull her round to the light that he may see her face. It is but a moment before the other passion of remorse comes to make havoc of the helpless child, and the first passion of anger is quelled outright.

Only to a trivial eye is there nothing tragic in the sight of these great passions within the small frame, the small will, and, in a word, the small nature. When a large and sombre fate befalls a little nature, and the stage is too narrow for the action of a tragedy, the disproportion has sometimes made a mute and unexpressed history of actual life or sometimes a famous book; it is the manifest core of George Eliot's story of "Adam Bede," where the suffering of Hetty is, as it were, the eye of the storm. All is expressive around her, but she is hardly articulate; the book is full of words—preachings, speeches, daily talk, aphorisms, but a space of silence remains about her in the midst of the story. And the disproportion of passion—the inner disproportion—is at least as tragic as that disproportion of fate and action; it is less intelligible, and leads into the intricacies of nature which are more difficult than the turn of events.

It seems, then, that this passionate play is acted within the narrow limits of a child's nature far oftener than in a nature adult and finally formed. And this, evidently, because there is unequal force at work within a child, unequal growth and a jostling of powers and energies that are hurrying to their development and pressing for exercise and life. It is this help-less inequality—this untimeliness—that makes the guileless comedy mingling with the tragedies of a poor child's day. He knows thus much—that life is troubled around him and that the fates are strong. He implicitly confesses "the strong hours" of antique song. This same boy—the tempestuous child of passion and revolt —went out with quiet cheerfulness for a walk lately, saying as his cap was put on, "Now, mother, you are going to have a little peace." This way of accepting his own conditions is shared by a sister, a very little older, who, being of an equal and gentle temper, indis-posed to violence of every kind and tender to all with-out disquiet, observes the boy's brief frenzies as a citizen observes the climate. She knows the signs quite well and can at any time give the explanation of some particular outburst, but without any attempt to go in search of further or more original causes. Still less is she moved by the virtuous indignation that is the least charming of the ways of some little girls. *Elle ne fait que constater.* Her equanimity has never been overset by the wildest of his moments, and she has witnessed them all. It is needless to say that she is not frightened by his drama, for Nature takes care that her young creatures shall not be injured by sympathies. Nature encloses them in the innocent indifference that pre-serves their brains from the more harassing kinds of distress.

Even the very frenzy of rage does not long dim or depress the boy. It is his repentance that makes him pale, and Nature here has been rather forced, perhaps

—with no very good result. Often must a mother wish that she might for a few years govern her child (as far as he is governable) by the lowest motives— trivial punishments and paltry rewards— rather than by any kind of appeal to his sensibilities. She would wish to keep the words "right" and "wrong" away from his childish ears, but in this she is not seconded by her lieutenants. The child himself is quite willing to close with her plans, in so far as he is able, and is reasonably interested in the results of her experiments. He wishes her attempts in his regard to have a fair chance. "Let's hope I'll be good all to-morrow," he says with the peculiar cheerfulness of his ordinary voice. "I do hope so, old man." "Then I'll get my penny. Mother, I was only naughty once yesterday; if I have only one naughtiness to-morrow, will you give me a half-penny?" "No reward except for real goodness all day long." "All right."

It is only too probable that this system (adopted only after the failure of other ways of reform) will be greatly disapproved as one of bribery. It may, however, be curiously inquired whether all kinds of reward might not equally be burlesqued by that word, and whether any government, spiritual or civil, has ever even professed to deny rewards. Moreover, those who would not give a child a penny for being good will not hesitate to fine him a penny for being naughty, and rewards and punishments must stand or fall together. The more logical objection will be that goodness is ideally the normal condition, and that it should have, therefore, no explicit extraordinary result, whereas naughtiness, being abnormal, should have a visible and unusual sequel. To this the rewarding mother may reply that it is not reasonable to take " goodness " in a little child of strong passions as the normal condition. The natural thing for him is to give full sway to impulses that are so violent as to overbear his powers.

But, after all, the controversy returns to the point of practice. What is the thought, or threat, or promise that will stimulate the weak will of the child, in the moment of rage and anger, to make a sufficient resistance? If the will were naturally as well developed as the passions, the stand would be soon made and soon successful; but as it is there must needs be a bracing by the suggestion of joy or fear. Let, then, the stimulus be of a mild and strong kind at once, and mingled with the thought of distant pleasure. To meet the suffering of rage and frenzy by the suffering of fear is assuredly to make of the little unquiet mind a battle-place of feelings too hurtfully tragic. The penny is mild and strong at once, with its still distant but certain joys of purchase; the promise and hope break the mood of misery, and the will takes heart to resist and conquer.

It is only in the lesser naughtiness that he is master of himself. The lesser the evil fit the more deliberate. So that his mother, knowing herself to be not greatly feared, once tried to mimic the father's voice with a menacing, " What 's that noise? " The child was persistently crying and roaring on an upper floor, in contumacy against his French nurse, when the barytone and threatening question was sent pealing up the stairs. The child was heard to pause and listen and then to say to his nurse, " *Ce n'est pas Monsieur ; c'est Madame,*" and then, without further loss of time, to resume the interrupted clamours.

Obviously, with a little creature of six years, there are two things mainly to be done—to keep the delicate brain from the evil of the present excitement, especially the excitement of painful feeling, and to break the habit of passion. Now that we know how certainly the special cells of the brain which are locally affected by pain and anger become hypertrophied by so much use, and all too ready for use in the future at the slightest stimulus, we can no longer slight the importance of habit. Any means, then, that can succeed in separating a little child from the habit of anger does fruitful work for him in the helpless time of his childhood. The work is not easy, but a little thought should make it easy for the elders to avoid the provocation which they—who should ward off provocations—are apt to bring about by sheer carelessness. It is only in childhood that our race knows such physical abandonment to sorrow and tears, as a child's despair; and the theatre with us must needs copy childhood if it would catch the note and action of a creature without hope.

THE CHILD OF SUBSIDING
TUMULT

THERE is a certain year that is winged, as it were, against the flight of time; it does so move, and yet withstands time's movement. It is full of pauses that are due to the energy of change, has bounds and rebounds, and when it is most active then it is longest. It is not long with languor. It has room for remoteness, and leisure for oblivion. It takes great excursions against time, and travels so as to enlarge its hours. This certain year is any one of the early years of fully conscious life, and therefore it is of all the dates. The Child of Tumult has been living amply and changefully through such a year—his eighth. It is difficult to believe that his is a year of the self-same date as that of the adult, the men who do not breast their days.

For them is the inelastic, or but slightly elastic, movement of things. Month matched with month shov·s a fairly equal length. Men and women never travel far from yesterday; nor is their morrow in a distant light. There is recognition and familiarity between their seasons. But the Child of Tumult has infinite prospects in his year. Forgetfulness and surprise set his east and west at immeasurable distance. His Lethe runs in the cheerful sun. You look on your own little adult year, and in imagination enlarge it, because you know it to be the contemporary of his. Even she who is quite old, if she have a vital fancy, may face a strange and great extent of a few years of her life still to come—his years, the years she is to live at his side.

Reason seems to be making good her rule in this little boy's life, not so much by slow degrees as by sudden and fitful accessions. His speech is yet so childish that he chooses, for a toy, with blushes of pleasure, "a little duck what can walk"; but with a beautifully clear accent he greets his mother with the colloquial question, "Well, darling, do you know the latest?" "The *what?*" "The latest: do you know the latest?" And then he tells his news, generally, it must be owned, with some reference to his own wrongs. On another occasion the unexpected little phrase was varied; the news of the war then raging distressed him; a thousand of the side he favoured had fallen. The child then came to his mother's room with the question: "Have you heard the saddest?" Moreover the "saddest" caused him several fits of perfectly silent tears, which seized him during the day, on his walks or at other moments of recollection. From such great causes arise such little things! Some of his grief was for the nation he admired, and some was for the triumph of his brother, whose sympathies were on the other side, and who perhaps did not spare his sensibilities.

The tumults of a little child's passions of anger and grief, growing fewer as he grows older, rather increase than lessen in their painfulness. There is a fuller consciousness of complete capitulation of all the

childish powers to the overwhelming compulsion of
anger. This is not temptation; the word is too weak
for the assault of a child's passion upon his will. That
little will is taken captive entirely, and before the
child was seven he knew that it was so. Such a consciousness leaves all babyhood behind and condemns
the child to suffer. For a certain passage of his life he
is neither unconscious of evil, as he was, nor strong
enough to resist it, as he will be. The time of the
subsiding of the tumult is by no means the least
pitiable of the phases of human life. Happily the recovery from each trouble is ready and sure; so that the
child who had been abandoned to naughtiness with
all his will in an entire consent to the gloomy possession of his anger, and who had later undergone a
haggard repentance, has his captivity suddenly turned
again, "like rivers in the south." "Forget it," he had
wept, in a kind of extremity of remorse: "forget it,
darling, and don't, don't be sad"; and it is he, happily,
who forgets. The wasted look of his pale face is
effaced by the touch of a single cheerful thought, and
five short minutes can restore the ruin, as though a
broken little German town should in the twinkling of
an eye be restored as no architect could restore it—
should be made fresh, strong, and tight again, looking
like a full box of toys, as a town was wont to look in
the new days of old.

When his ruthless angers are not in possession the
child shows the growth of this tardy reason that—
quickened—is hereafter to do so much for his peace
and dignity, by the sweetest consideration. Denied a
second handful of strawberries, and seeing quite clearly

that the denial was enforced reluctantly, he makes haste to reply, "It doesn't matter, darling." At any sudden noise in the house his beautiful voice, with all its little difficulties of pronunciation, is heard with the sedulous reassurance: "It's all right, mother, nobody hurted ourselves!" He is not surprised so as to forget this gentle little duty, which was never required of him, but is of his own devising.

According to the opinion of his dear and admired American friend, he says all these things, good and evil, with an English accent; and at the American play his English accent was irrepressible. "It's too comic; no, it's too comic," he called in his enjoyment; being the only perfectly fearless child in the world, he will not consent to the conventional shyness in public, whether he be the member of an audience or of a congregation, but makes himself perceptible. And even when he has a desperate thing to say, in the moment of absolute revolt—such a thing as "I *can't* like you, mother," which anon he will recant with convulsions of distress—he has to "speak the thing he will," and when he recants it is not for fear.

If such a child could be ruled (or approximately ruled, for inquisitorial government could hardly be so much as attempted) by some small means adapted to his size and to his physical aspect, it would be well for his health, but that seems at times impossible. By no effort can his elders altogether succeed in keeping tragedy out of the life that is so unready for it. Against great emotions no one can defend him by any forethought. He is their subject; and to see him thus devoted and thus wrung, thus wrecked by tempests inwardly, so that you feel grief has him actually by the heart, recalls the reluctance—the question—wherewith you perceive the interior grief of poetry or of a devout life. Cannot the Muse, cannot the Saint, you ask, live with something less than this? If this is the truer life, it seems hardly supportable. In like manner it should be possible for a child of seven to come through his childhood with griefs that should not so closely involve him, but should deal with the easier sentiments.

Despite all his simplicity, the child has (by way of inheritance, for he has never heard them) the self-excusing fictions of our race. Accused of certain acts of violence, and unable to rebut the charge with any effect, he flies to the old convention: "I didn't know what I was doing," he avers, using a great deal of gesticulation to express the temporary distraction of his mind. "Darling, after nurse slapped me as hard as she could, I didn't know what I was doing, so I suppose I pushed her with my foot." His mother knows as well as does Tolstoi that men and children know what they are doing, and are the more intently aware as the stress of feeling makes the moments more tense; and she will not admit a plea which her child might have learned from the undramatic authors he has never read.

Far from repenting of her old system of rewards, and far from taking fright at the name of a bribe, the mother of the Child of Tumult has only to wish she had at command rewards ample and varied enough to give the shock of hope and promise to the heart of her little boy, and change his passion at its height.

THE UNREADY

I T is rashly said that the senses of children are quick.
They are, on the contrary, unwieldy in turning,
unready in reporting, until advancing age teaches them
agility. This is not lack of sensitiveness, but mere length
of process. For instance, a child nearly newly born is
cruelly startled by a sudden crash in the room,—a child
who has never learnt to fear, and is merely overcome
by the shock of sound; nevertheless, that shock of sound
does not reach the conscious hearing or the nerves but
after some moments, nor before some moments more is
the sense of the shock expressed. The sound travels to
the remoteness and seclusion of the child's consciousness,
as the roar of a gun travels to listeners half a mile away.

So it is, too, with pain, which has learnt to be so instant and eager with us of later age that no point of
time is lost in its touches—direct as the unintercepted
message of great and candid eyes, unhampered by
trivialities; even so immediate is the communication or
pain. But you could count five between the prick of a
surgeon's instrument upon a baby's arm and the little
whimper that answers it. The child is then too young,
also, to refer the feeling of pain to the arm that suffers
it. Even when pain has groped its way to his mind it
hardly seems to bring local tidings thither. The baby
does not turn his eyes in any degree towards his arm or
towards the side that is so vexed with vaccination. He

looks in any other direction at haphazard, and cries at random.

See, too, how slowly the unpractised apprehension of an older child trudges after the nimbleness of a conjurer. It is the greatest failure to take these little *gobe-mouches* to a good conjurer. His successes leave them cold, for they had not yet understood what it was the good man meant to surprise them withal. The amateur it is who really astonishes them. They cannot come up even with your amateur beginner performing at close quarters; whereas the master of his craft on a platform runs quite away at the outset from the lagging senses of his honest audience.

You may rob a child of his dearest plate at table, almost from under his ingenuous eyes, send him off in chase of it, and have it in its place and off again ten times before the little breathless boy has begun to perceive in what direction his sweets have been snatched.

Teachers of young children should therefore teach themselves a habit of awaiting, should surround themselves with pauses of patience. The simple little processes of logic that arrange the grammar of a common sentence are too quick for these young blunderers, who cannot use two pronouns but they must confuse them. I never found that a young child—one of something under nine years—was able to say, "I send them my love" at the first attempt. It will be "I send me my love," "I send them their love," "They send me my love"; not, of course, through any confusion of understanding, but because of the tardy setting of words in order with the thoughts. The child visibly grapples with the difficulty, and is beaten.

It is no doubt this unreadiness that causes little children to like twice-told tales and foregone conclusions in their games. They are not eager, for a year or two yet to come, for surprises. If you hide and they cannot see you hiding, their joy in finding you is comparatively small; but let them know perfectly well what cupboard you are in, and they will find you with shouts of discovery. The better the hiding-place is understood between you the more lively the drama. They make a convention of art for their play. The younger the children the more dramatic; and when the house is filled with outcries of laughter from the breathless breast of a child, it is that he is pretending to be surprised at finding his mother where he bade her pretend to hide. This is the comedy that never tires. Let the elder who cannot understand its charm beware how he tries to put a more intelligible form of delight in the place of it; for, if not, he will find that children also have a manner of substitution, and that they will put half-hearted laughter in the place of their natural impetuous clamours. It is certain that very young children like to play upon their own imaginations, and enjoy their own short game.

There is something so purely childlike in the delays of a child that any exercise asking for the swift apprehension of later life, for the flashes of understanding and action, from the mind and members of childhood, is no pleasure to see. The piano, for instance, as experts understand it, and even as the moderately-trained may play it, claims all the immediate action, the instantaneousness, most unnatural to childhood. There may possibly be feats of skill to which young children could be trained without this specific violence directed upon the thing characteristic of their age—their unreadiness— but virtuosity at the piano cannot be one of them. It is no delight, indeed, to see the shyness of children, or anything that is theirs, conquered and beaten; but their poor little slowness is so distinctively their own, and must needs be physiologically so proper to their years, so much a natural condition of the age of their brain, that of all childishnesses it is the one that the world should have the intelligence to understand, the patience to attend upon, and the humanity to foster.

It is true that the movements of young children are quick, but a very little attention would prove how many apparent disconnexions there are between the lively motion and the first impulse; it is not the brain that is quick. If, on a voyage in space, electricity takes thus much time, and light thus much, and sound thus much, there is one little jogging traveller that would arrive after the others had forgotten their journey, and this is the perception of a child. Surely our own memories might serve to remind us how in our childhood we in- evitably missed the principal point in any procession or pageant intended by our elders to furnish us with a historical remembrance for the future. It was not our mere vagueness of understanding, it was the unwieldi- ness of our senses, of our reply to the suddenness of the grown up. We lived through the important moments of the passing of an Emperor at a different rate from theirs; we stared long in the wake of his Majesty, and of anything else of interest; every flash of movement, that got telegraphic answers from our parents' eyes, left us stragglers. We fell out of all ranks. Among the sights proposed for our instruction, that which befitted us best was an eclipse of the moon, done at leisure. In good time we found the moon in the sky, in good time the eclipse set in and made reasonable progress; we kept up with everything.

It is too often required of children that they should adjust themselves to the world, practised and alert. But it would be more to the purpose that the world should adjust itself to children in all its dealings with them. Those who run and keep together have to run at the pace of the tardiest. But we are apt to command instant obedience, stripped of the little pauses that a child, while very young, cannot act without. It is not a child of ten or twelve that needs them so; it is the young creature who has but lately ceased to be a baby, slow to be startled.

We have but to consider all that it implies of the loitering of senses and of an unprepared consciousness —this capacity for receiving a great shock from a noise and this perception of the shock after two or three appreciable moments—if we would know anything of the moments of a baby.

Even as we must learn that our time, when it is long, is too long for children, so must we learn that our time, when it is short, is too short for them. When it is exceedingly short they cannot, without an unnatural effort, have any perception of it. When children do not see the jokes of the elderly, and disappoint expectation in other ways, only less intimate, the reason is almost always there. The child cannot turn in mid-career; he goes fast, but the impetus took place moments ago.

THAT PRETTY PERSON

DURING the many years in which "evolution" was the favourite word, one significant lesson—so it seems—was learnt, which has outlived controversy, and has remained longer than the questions at issue—an interesting and unnoticed thing cast up by the storm of thoughts. This is a disposition, a general consent, to find the use and the value of process, and even to understand a kind of repose in the very wayfaring of progress. With this is a resignation to change, and something more than resignation—a delight in those qualities that could not be but for their transitoriness.

What, then, is this but the admiration, at last confessed by the world, for childhood? Time was when childhood was but borne with, and that for the sake of its mere promise of manhood. We do not now hold, perhaps, that promise so high. Even, nevertheless, if we held it high, we should acknowledge the approach to be a state adorned with its own conditions.

But it was not so once. As the primitive lullaby is nothing but a patient prophecy (the mother's), so was education, some two hundred years ago, nothing but an impatient prophecy (the father's) of the full stature of body and mind. The Indian woman sings of the future hunting. If her song is not restless, it is because she has a sense of the results of time, and has submitted her heart to experience. Childhood is a time of danger; "Would it were done." But, meanwhile, the right thing is to put it to sleep and guard its slumbers. It will pass. She sings prophecies to the child of his hunting, as she sings a song about the robe while she spins, and a song about bread as she grinds corn. She bids good speed.

John Evelyn was equally eager, and not so submissive. His child—"that pretty person" in Jeremy Taylor's letter of condolence—was chiefly precious to him inasmuch as he was, too soon, a likeness of the man he never lived to be. The father, writing with tears when the boy was dead, says of him: "At two and a half years of age he pronounced English, Latin, and French exactly, and could perfectly read in these three languages." As he lived precisely five years, all he did was done at that little age, and it comprised this: "He got by heart almost the entire vocabulary of Latin and French primitives and words, could make congruous syntax, turn English into Latin, and *vice versa*, construe and prove what he read, and did the government and use of relatives, verbs, substantives, ellipses, and many figures and tropes, and made a considerable progress in Comenius's ' Janua,' and had a strong passion for Greek."

Grant that this may be a little abated, because a very serious man is not to be too much believed when he is describing what he admires; it is the very fact of his admiration that is so curious a sign of those hasty times. All being favourable, the child of Evelyn's studious home would have done all these things in the course of nature within a few years. It was the fact that he did them out of the course of nature that was, to Evelyn, so exquisite. The course of nature had not any beauty in his eyes. It might be borne with for the sake of the end, but it was not admired for the majesty of its unhasting process. Jeremy Taylor mourns with him " the strangely hopeful child," who —without Comenius's " Janua " and without congruous syntax—was fulfilling, had they known it, an appropriate hope, answering a distinctive prophecy, and crowning and closing a separate expectation every day of his five years.

Ah! the word "hopeful" seems, to us, in this day, a word too flattering to the estate of man. They thought their little boy strangely hopeful because he was so quick on his way to be something else. They lost the timely perfection the while they were so intent upon their hopes. And yet it is our own modern age that is charged with haste!

It would seem rather as though the world, whatever it shall unlearn, must rightly learn to confess the passing and irrevocable hour; not slighting it, or bidding it hasten its work, not yet hailing it, with Faust, " Stay, thou art so fair!" Childhood is but change made gay and visible, and the world has lately been converted to change.

Our fathers valued change for the sake of its results; we value it in the act. To us the change is revealed as perpetual; every passage is a goal, and every goal a passage. The hours are equal; but some of them wear apparent wings.

Tout passe. Is the fruit for the flower, or the flower for the fruit, or the fruit for the seeds which it is formed to shelter and contain? It seems as though our forefathers had answered this question most arbitrarily as to the life of man.

All their literature dealing with children is bent upon this haste, this suppression of the approach to what seemed then the only time of fulfilment. The way was without rest to them. And this because they had the illusion of a rest to be gained at some later point of this unpausing life.

Evelyn and his contemporaries dropped the very word child as soon as might be, if not sooner. When a poor little boy came to be eight years old they called him a youth. The diarist himself had no cause to be proud of his own early years, for he was so far indulged in idleness by an " honoured grandmother " that he was " not initiated into any rudiments " till he was four years of age. He seems even to have been a youth of eight before Latin was seriously begun; but this fact he is evidently, in after years, with a total lack of a sense of humour, rather ashamed of, and hardly acknowledges. It is difficult to imagine what childhood must have been when nobody, looking on, saw any fun in it; when everything that was proper to five years old was defect. A strange good conceit of themselves and of their own ages had those fathers.

They took their children seriously, without relief. Evelyn has nothing to say about his little ones that has a sign of a smile in it. Twice are children not his own mentioned in his diary. Once he goes to the wedding of a maid of five years old—a curious thing, but not, evidently, an occasion of sensibility. Another time he stands by, in a French hospital, while a youth

of less than nine years of age undergoes a frightful
surgical operation "with extraordinary patience." "The
use I made of it was to give Almighty God hearty
thanks that I had not been subject to this deplorable
infirmitie." This is what he says.

See, moreover, how the fashion of hurrying childhood prevailed in literature, and how it abolished little
girls. It may be that there were in all ages—even
those—certain few boys who insisted upon being
children; whereas the girls were docile to the adult
ideal. Art, for example, had no little girls. There was
always Cupid, and there were the prosperous urchin-
angels of the painters; the one who is hauling up his
little brother by the hand in the "Last Communion
of St. Jerome" might be called Tommy. But there
were no "little radiant girls." Now and then an
"Education of the Virgin" is the exception, and then
it is always a matter of sewing and reading. As for the
little girl saints, even when they were so young that
their hands, like those of St. Agnes, slipped through
their fetters, they are always recorded as refusing importunate suitors, which seems necessary to make them
interesting to the mediaeval mind, but mars them for
ours.

So does the hurrying and ignoring of little-girl-child-
hood somewhat hamper the delight with which readers
of John Evelyn admire his most admirable Mrs. Go-
dolphin. She was Maid of Honour to the Queen in
the Court of Charles II. She was, as he prettily says,
an Arethusa "who passed through all those turbulent
waters without so much as the least stain or tincture
in her christall." She held her state with men and

maids for her servants, guided herself by most exact
rules, such as that of never speaking to the King, gave
an excellent example and instruction to the other maids
of honour, was " severely careful how she might give the
least countenance to that liberty which the gallants
there did usually assume," refused the addresses of the
" greatest persons," and was as famous for her beauty
as for her wit. One would like to forget the age at
which she did these things. When she began her service she was eleven. When she was making her rule
never to speak to the King she was not thirteen.

Marriage was the business of daughters of fourteen
and fifteen, and heroines, therefore, were of those ages.
The poets turned April into May, and seemed to think
that they lent a grace to the year if they shortened
and abridged the spring of their many songs. The particular year they sang of was to be a particularly fine
year, as who should say a fine child and forward, with
congruous syntax at two years old, and ellipses, figures,
and tropes. Even as late as Keats a poet would not
have patience with the process of the seasons, but
boasted of untimely flowers. The "musk-rose" is
never in fact the child of mid-May, as he has it.

The young women of Addison are nearly fourteen
years old. His fear of losing the idea of the bloom of
their youth makes him so tamper with the bloom of
their childhood. The young heiress of seventeen in the
"Spectator" has looked upon herself as marriageable
" for the last six years." The famous letter describing
the figure, the dance, the wit, the stockings of the
charming Mr. Shapely is supposed to be written by a
girl of thirteen, " willing to settle in the world as soon

as she can." She adds, " I have a good portion which they cannot hinder me of." This correspondent is one of " the women who seldom ask advice before they have bought their wedding clothes." There was no sense of childhood in an age that could think this an opportune pleasantry.

But impatience of the way and the wayfaring was to disappear from a later century—an age that has found all things to be on a journey, and all things complete in their day because it is their day, and has its appointed end. It is the tardy conviction of this, rather than a sentiment ready made, that has caused the childhood of children to seem, at last, something else than a defect.

UNDER THE EARLY STARS

PLAY is not for every hour of the day, or for any hour taken at random. There is a tide in the affairs of children. Civilization is cruel in sending them to bed at the most stimulating time of dusk. Summer dusk, especially, is the frolic moment for children, baffle them how you may. They may have been in a pottering mood all day, intent upon all kinds of close industries, breathing hard over choppings and poundings. But when late twilight comes, there comes also the punctual wildness. The children will run and pursue, and laugh for the mere movement—it does so jolt their spirits.

What remembrances does this imply of the hunt, what of the predatory dark? The kitten grows alert at the same hour, and hunts for moths and crickets in the grass. It comes like an imp, leaping on all fours. The children lie in ambush and fall upon one another in the mimicry of hunting.

The sudden outbreak of action is complained of as a defiance and a rebellion. Their entertainers are tired, and the children are to go home. But, with more or less of life and fire, the children strike some blow for liberty. It may be the impotent revolt of the ineffectual child, or the stroke of the conqueror; but something, something is done for freedom under the early stars.

This is not the only time when the energy of

children is in conflict with the weariness of men. But it is less tolerable that the energy of men should be at odds with the weariness of children, which happens at some time of their jaunts together, especially, alas! in the jaunts of the poor.

Of games for the summer dusk when it rains, cards are most beloved by children. Three tiny girls were to be taught "old maid" to beguile the time. One of them, a nut-brown child of five, was persuading another to play. "Oh come," she said, "and play with me at new maid,"

The time of falling asleep is a child's immemorial and incalculable hour. It is full of traditions, and beset by antique habits. The habit of prehistoric races has been cited as the only explanation of the fixity of some customs in mankind. But if the inquirers who appeal to that beginning remembered better their own infancy, they would seek no further. See the habits in falling to sleep which have children in their thralldom. Try to overcome them in any child, and his own conviction of their high antiquity weakens your hand.

Childhood is antiquity, and with the sense of time and the sense of mystery is connected for ever the hearing of a lullaby. The French sleep-song is the most romantic. There is in it such a sound of history as must inspire any imaginative child, falling to sleep, with a sense of the incalculable; and the songs themselves are old. "Le Bon Roi Dagobert" has been sung over French cradles since the legend was fresh. The nurse knows nothing more sleepy than the tune and the verse that she herself slept to when a child. The gaiety of the thirteenth century, in "Le Pont d'Avignon," is put mysteriously to sleep, away in the *tête à tête* of child and nurse, in a thousand little sequestered rooms at night. " Malbrook " would be comparatively modern, were not all things that are sung to a drowsing child as distant as the day of Abraham.

If English children are not rocked to many such aged lullabies, some of them are put to sleep to strange cradle-songs. The affectionate races that are brought into subjection sing the primitive lullaby to the white child. Asiatic voices and African persuade him to sleep in the tropical night. His closing eyes are filled with alien images.

THE ILLUSION OF HISTORIC
TIME

HE who has survived his childhood intelligently
must become conscious of something more than
a change in his sense of the present and in his apprehension of the future. He must be aware of no less a
thing than the destruction of the past. Its events and
empires stand where they did, and the mere relation of
time is as it was. But that which has fallen together,
has fallen in, has fallen close, and lies in a little heap,
is the past itself—time—the fact of antiquity.

He has grown into a smaller world as he has grown
older. There are no more extremities. Recorded time
has no more terrors. The unit of measure which he
holds in his hand has become in his eyes a thing of
paltry length. The discovery draws in the annals of
mankind. He had thought them to be wide.

For a man has nothing whereby to order and place
the floods, the states, the conquests, and the temples of
the past, except only the measure which he holds. Call
that measure a space of ten years. His first ten years
had given him the illusion of a most august scale and
measure. It was then that he conceived Antiquity.
But now! Is it to a decade of ten such little years as
these now in his hand—ten of his mature years—that
men give the dignity of a century? They call it an

age; but what if life shows now so small that the word age has lost its gravity?

In fact, when a child begins to know that there is a past, he has a most noble rod to measure it by—he has his own ten years. He attributes an overwhelming majesty to all recorded time. He confers distance. He, and he alone, bestows mystery. Remoteness is his. He creates more than mortal centuries. He sends armies fighting into the extremities of the past. He assigns the Parthenon to a hill of ages, and the temples of Upper Egypt to sidereal time.

If there were no child, there would be nothing old. He, having conceived old time, communicates a remembrance at least of the mystery to the mind of the man. The man perceives at last all the illusion, but he cannot forget what was his conviction when he was a child. He had once a persuasion of Antiquity. And this is not for nothing. The enormous undeception that comes upon him still leaves spaces in his mind.

But the undeception is rude work. The man receives successive shocks. It is as though one strained level eyes towards the horizon, and then were bidden to shorten his sight and to close his search within a poor half acre before his face. Now, it is that he suddenly perceives the hitherto remote, remote youth of his own parents to have been something familiarly near, so measured by his new standard; again, it is the coming of Attila that is displaced. Those ten last years of his have corrected the world. There needs no other rod than that ten years' rod to chastise all the imaginations of the spirit of man. It makes history skip.

To have lived through any appreciable part of any

century is to hold thenceforth a mere century cheap enough. But, it may be said, the mystery of change remains. Nay, it does not. Change that trudges through our own world—our contemporary world—is not very mysterious. We perceive its pace; it is a jog-trot. Even so, we now consider, jolted the changes of the past, with the same hurry.

The man, therefore, who has intelligently ceased to be a child scans through a shortened avenue the reaches of the past. He marvels that he was so deceived. For it was a very deception. If the Argonauts, for instance, had been children, it would have been well enough for the child to measure their remoteness and their acts with his own magnificent measure. But they were only men and demi-gods. Thus they belong to him as he is now—a man; and not to him as he was once— a child. It was quite wrong to lay the child's enormous ten years' rule along the path from our time to theirs; that path must be skipped by the nimble yard in the man's present possession. Decidedly the Argonauts are no subject for the boy.

What, then? Is the record of the race nothing but a bundle of such little times? Nay, it seems that childhood, which created the illusion of ages, does actually prove it true. Childhood is itself Antiquity—to every man his only Antiquity. The recollection of childhood cannot make Abraham old again in the mind of a man of thirty-five; but the beginning of every life is older than Abraham. *There* is the abyss of time. Let a man turn to his own childhood—no further—if he would renew his sense of remoteness, and of the mystery of change.

For in childhood change does not go at that mere hasty amble; it rushes; but it has enormous space for its flight. The child has an apprehension not only of things far off, but of things far apart; an illusive apprehension when he is learning "ancient" history—a real apprehension when he is conning his own immeasurable infancy. If there is no historical Antiquity worth speaking of, this is the renewed and unnumbered Antiquity for all mankind.

And it is of this—merely of this—that "ancient" history seems to partake. Rome was founded when we began Roman history, and that is why it seems long ago. Suppose the man of thirty-five heard, at that present age, for the first time of Romulus. Why, Romulus would be nowhere. But he built his wall, as a matter of fact, when every one was seven years old. It is by good fortune that "ancient" history is taught in the only ancient days. So, for a time, the world is magical.

Modern history does well enough for learning later. But by learning something of antiquity in the first ten years, the child enlarges the sense of time for all mankind. For even after the great illusion is over and history is re-measured, and all fancy and flight caught back and chastised, the enlarged sense remains enlarged. The man remains capable of great spaces of time. He will not find them in Egypt, it is true, but he finds them within, he contains them, he is aware of them. History has fallen together, but childhood surrounds and encompasses history, stretches beyond and passes on the road to eternity.

He has not passed in vain through the long ten years,

the ten years that are the treasury of preceptions—the first. The great disillusion shall never shorten those years, nor set nearer together the days that made them. "Far apart," I have said, and that "far apart" is wonderful. The past of childhood is not single, is not motionless, nor fixed in one point; it has summits a world away one from the other. Year from year differs as the antiquity of Mexico from the antiquity of Chaldea. And the man of thirty-five knows for ever afterwards what is flight, even though he finds no great historic distances to prove his wings by.

There is a long and mysterious moment in long and mysterious childhood, which is the extremest distance known to any human fancy. Many other moments, many other hours, are long in the first ten years. Hours of weariness are long—not with a mysterious length, but with a mere length of protraction, so that the things called minutes and half-hours by the elderly may be something else to their apparent contemporaries, the children. The ancient moment is not merely one of these—it is a space not of long, but of immeasurable, time. It is the moment of going to sleep. The man knows that borderland, and has a contempt for it: he has long ceased to find antiquity there. It has become a common enough margin of dreams to him; and he does not attend to its phantasies. He knows that he has a frolic spirit in his head which has its way at those hours, but he is not interested in it. It is the inexperienced child who passes with simplicity through the marginal country; and the thing he meets there is principally the yet further conception of illimitable time.

His nurse's lullaby is translated into the mysteries of time. She sings absolutely immemorial words. It matters little what they may mean to waking ears; to the ears of a child going to sleep they tell of the beginning of the world. He has fallen asleep to the sound of them all his life; and "all his life" means more than older speech can well express.

Ancient custom is formed in a single spacious year. A child is beset with long traditions. And his infancy is so old, so old, that the mere adding of years in the life to follow will not seem to throw it further back— it is already so far. That is, it looks as remote to the memory of a man of thirty as to that of a man of seventy. For what are a mere forty years of added later life in the contemplation of such a distance?